INDEPENDENTLY SERIES

Independently Foolish
Independently Raised
Coming Soon Independently
Loved & Independently Moved

Independently Raised

Neglected, Forgotten & Underestimated

DR. ERIKA JONES, BA, MPA, PH.D.

authorHOUSE®

AuthorHouse™
1663 Liberty Drive
Bloomington, IN 47403
www.authorhouse.com
Phone: 833-262-8899

Published by AuthorHouse 01/14/2021

ISBN: 978-1-6655-1372-2 (sc)
ISBN: 978-1-6655-1371-5 (e)

Dedication

This book is dedicated to my three
beautiful daughters Daizha, Zuri,
Zoey, and my bonus daughter Jarah.
I want you all to know that I work
really hard in life to beat the odds
and I can only hope to serve as a role
model for you to stand up for what you
believe in and chase your dreams.

Acknowledgments

I want to thank Mr. Jared Washington, Sr. for having the patience to allow me to heal from all the pain that had absolutely nothing to do with him, and still love me unconditionally. You have helped me in so many ways. Your ideas and thoughts were useful while writing. I appreciate you for wanting to help me heal and waiting for me to be ready to fully love again. You never gave up on me and after 20 years of chasing after me, I owe my loyalty to you. I love you with all my heart. You are truly one of a kind.

Contents

Introduction

Many people have grown up with divorced or separated parents, and I am positive that many more to come will. When I grew up my mother stopped her dreams of being a flight attendant to actually raise the children, and my father pursued his dream career. My father was in the military and later became a United States Marshall. I always looked up to him for being really successful and although his presence was not there, financially he did take care of his children. I was born and raised in the south suburbs of Chicago, Illinois. Anyone who is from Chicago automatically becomes resilient and ready for war! A Chicagoan can survive absolutely anywhere, and being raised here helped me become quick on my feet. I am happy that I was raised in Chicago because it made me tough. My life is probably beyond complicated, and I have been through a lot that no one knew. I am a very private person and it is hard for me to come out of my shell. But, for the purposes of helping someone else, I prefer to share my story because I am the true definition of Independently Raised. Don't get it twisted, I do have wonderful parents but, I have always been the child who grew up unaccompanied, always alone, with my own mind, and creatively built myself up.

Unfortunately

From the time I remembered, my parents were divorced. I was a baby when they separated and this is an occurrence I couldn't remember because I was under one years old. But, that was the very moment my life changed forever, and I truly had no clue. I don't think when parents separate they think of the aftermath. It is an old saying that states that when one parent leaves the home, typically not always, it is the father, but it is said that they left your mama, not you. But, that is the furthest thing from the truth. In reality, they left you as well. Even the best co-parent team out here will never get the every single day life spent with their child once separation begins. As a culture, we forget how having a strong black family is important. It really is a very important topic that should be explored more in-depth. It is ignored and repeated generation after generation. A very bad generational cycle.

I am always amazed to see two people who were once in love at one point, separate and hate each other not too soon thereafter. Makes me question was it real love in the beginning or was in all a lie? I know at some point my parents were extremely in love and although they did not grow to hate each other, my father's infidelity separated them. At least that was the story I was given by my mother, and later confirmed by my grandmother and my brother that was born right after me to another woman. Whatever happened with them, happened, but it forced us to move many times.

When my parents broke up we moved out of our house into an apartment. My mother struggled to pay the bills and decided to move out of state. We moved to Phoenix, Arizona because my mom wanted to have a change in environment. My father didn't want his three children to live in Arizona so we moved back to Illinois. I really wish we could have stayed out of state but we came back because we had no choice. It is rather funny he wanted us to come back because he end up moving to another state eventually forcing us to see less of him. After we came back from Arizona we end up staying in another apartment in Riverdale, Illinois which is a south suburb of Chicago. I met plenty of friends in that town that I still communicate with today.

What I remember about Riverdale was me joining girl scouts, meeting some really nice twins, and a girl who shared the same birthday as me. The twin's birthday was actually three days after me so often our parents would allow us to share the day. Since we shared the same friends it was very convenient. I also remember sharing all my birthday parties with my older brother Leroy. Leroy's birthday was 6 days before me so our mom would often make the birthday cakes half blue and half pink. She did her best to accommodate us and celebrate our birthdays. I knew she couldn't afford to have us separate parties, but I really wanted my own party. Unfortunately, that day never came. See, as a single mom she had to work all day and every day. She often had to leave her three children alone. There was no one to really watch us. This is one of those things that was normal for us, but there wasn't much she could do. At this time our dad was in the military, was newly married, and had two new sons.

He would always call for us and he even paid child support monthly. He provided us medical insurance as well. Most people would be happy with this type of support and trust me I am grateful, but as children, we don't see money, insurance, or even his efforts. All we see is he is not with us daily. My dad not being there physically and our mother having to work all the time has scarred all three of us in our own little way. For me, it created a level of resentment and pain that seem to never go away. Due to us always being alone, I experienced some things in life that I shouldn't have. I never really talked about some of this until now. I know that once my parents read this book they will be confused and might even be hurt but this is what happens to children when you decide to separate. I was fortunate to not ever been raped but I was touched inappropriately by one of my brother's friends. I was scared to tell anyone because I was threatened by him. I was told that they wouldn't believe me anyway. But crazily, he was right and there was no one there to protect me.

I was young, confused, so I laid there while he did what he wanted. He didn't know what he was doing either because he wasn't that much older and he didn't hurt me, he just fondled me. Now what I have learned is that most children born around the 80's played house. House was a game that someone would pretend to be the mother, father, and the rest were children. The parents would run around and whoop the children and it was a fun game until I was always the only girl. So I always had to be the mom. So since I was the mom, the father (who was my brother's friend) would always be ready to put the children to sleep so that he could bring me into a room and be the daddy, which meant he would climb on top of me and be grown. I think that he probably watched his own parents have sex and then it was normal for this type of activity. But, it wasn't right nor should it have happened to me. This made me not trust boys early on. Therefore, I was never a fast girl growing up.

My point of sharing these disturbing facts is to show parents that you think that you can protect your children from these things, but unless you keep an eye on your children 24/7, anything can happen to them. I hated playing house and I used to beg my mom to let me go over to my friend's home. Sometimes she would actually let me go. If I couldn't go to my friends, I would beg to go to my maternal grandmother's house. You think as a parent you are the best by providing for the children who you birthed, and this is essential but their well-being socially is just as important. You can be a millionaire and send your children all the money in the world, and it can happen to your children as well if you are not present.

Due to my mother working two jobs, sometimes three, she definitely did the very best she could do. After staying in Riverdale for a few years and seeing my father leave the state of Illinois, my mother moved us to the state she was born in and that was Mississippi. Yes, she took us south and I experienced all types of things while down there such as earthquakes, ringworms, mumps, chickenpox, eating pig feet, and even a pickle with a peppermint. However, the most important thing I learned was how to cook from scratch living with my Aunt T. She was one of those impressionable women who would whoop your butt, still love you to death, but make the world of difference in your life. Going to school down there was different too because I misbehaved in class one day, and my teacher whooped my butt. My teacher used a wooden paddle and tore my butt up, and called my mom to tell her. It was like she was bragging.

We didn't stay in Mississippi very long either. After a year, we went right back to Illinois but this time we stayed at my great grandad home in Markham, Illinois. Now there was always someone staying at this house. It was like a revolving door and there were many families living there at the same time. Now it wasn't the best house, nor was it the cleanest house. But it was a roof over our head. I shared a room with my brothers and my mom. We were crowded and we lived with roaches and mice. At this time of my life, I realized how poor we were. We didn't have our own home or own room. I despised my father more and more during this time because he had a lovely home and we didn't. He got married and moved on and had more children and I felt like he left us in hell. Now, I do not know if he asked my mom if we could reside with him and he may have, but my mom wasn't giving up her children because we were all she had. I realized my mom was heartbroken and miserable so I tried my best to be on my best behavior to not make her life any harder.

My mom started going out a lot and hanging out. I think this was part of her depression. She ended up getting a management position at Taco Bell. She used to pick us up from school and take us to work with her every day. We went to work with her and sat in a booth and ate Taco Bell every day. I had every toy in every happy meal, and we also went to sleep in that booth until she got off work. She worked 2nd shift so we were there to about 11:00 pm. We would go to our great grandfather's house, shower, and go to bed. Just to start all over again. This was our life and at least we were healthy, breathing, and living. I guess you can say, count your blessings.

Scars

My mom met a nice quiet guy who decided to buy her a car. All this time we didn't have a vehicle. I will never forget this car as it was a bright royal blue Geo Storm. My mom named it Betsey. But crazily, she names all her cars Betsey. We didn't have to take the bus, cab, or get a ride any longer. We were done walking everywhere when Betsey arrived. She married that nice man, but she didn't truly love him. Not like she loved my dad. I believe she married him for security purposes. He got us our own place and we moved out of our great grandfather's home for good.

The nice guy must have really loved blue because their entire wedding was royal blue as well. I really appreciated this man for giving us our own rooms. We were in a three-bedroom apartment and my mom had a car. My mom was happy to have our own space, but no matter how hard she tried, she just was not in love with this guy. He had a decent job and a little money, but he wasn't very attractive. He was not very easy on the eye and it was apparent by her annulment that she didn't want to marry him. But due to him paying for everything, my mom saved all her money to move out and get us our own apartment and we moved back to Riverdale. But this time when we moved, we lived on another side of town. She was working daily once again and it wasn't long before she met a new guy who wanted to marry her. My momma was foxy and a beautiful chocolate woman so she didn't have any trouble finding a man. She married her third husband who moved us to Dolton, Illinois. My mother was actually happy with her new husband and he was really nice to all of her children. We were no longer in an apartment. We were in a house and we even got our first pet which was a dog named River. I am not so positive what type of dog River was because I was about 8 years old. I was going to a new school for 3rd grade and I was excited. I had the biggest room in the house, even bigger than the master bedroom.

Now at this time, my father was reaching out to ask for us for a couple of weeks every summer. We would go visit him a couple of weeks and then to South Bend, Indiana for a few weeks to visit with our paternal grandmother for the summer. We traveled by train or car to see our grandmother. We used to have a ball down in Indiana with our grandparents, uncles, aunts, and many cousins. Just when things began to get normal and I was happy, I started to have trouble with my father growing up. I will explain this trouble because it caused a scar in my life. I was a dancer in school, you know the pom-poms and dance troop type of girl. I had many performances and my mom would make every single performance and I wanted my dad to be there. But, due to him living in another state, and his demanding career, it was difficult for him to make it. I started feeling like he wasn't a good dad. Now even though this wasn't true, I was young, and of course he was paying child support, but that didn't mean anything to me. But that is not where the scar began. I was hurt he was missing birthdays, holidays, and even all my performances. But, what changed me is one summer he was supposed to get us for a visit and he told me he couldn't afford it. While I was sad, I understood. I really wanted to visit my dad this one summer. But he said he couldn't afford it.

By this time, my dad had divorced my two younger brother's mom and was now married to my sister's mom. They were living in St. Thomas, Virgin Islands and he said it was extremely expensive to send three children down there which is understandable so I didn't make a big deal about it. But I did ask my mom to contact my two younger brothers who lived in Atlanta to tell them that dad wouldn't be getting us this summer and that I would miss them. When I called their mother said to me that they were not there and that they were indeed with my dad. I was very shocked and confused about this. I immediately called my dad back to ask him how he could take my two younger brothers and not my mom's three children. His response changed me forever. He said that it was easier to take two rather than three and that would mean 5 of us would be down there plus my sister. With my sister that would be 6 of his children. I know he thinks he was doing the right thing, but what he did at this very day, was push me into the direction of being young and foolish and that is exactly what happened thereafter.

I ran into my mother's bedroom and told her what happened. She tried to console me but, I was too upset. I cried myself to sleep and when I woke up the next day, I went downstairs and asked her husband could he be my father instead. That is how hurt I was and I felt alone and unprotected. Every daughter wants a father's love and protection, and I didn't feel like I had it. I know my dad always loved me but for this moment right here, I began looking for love. The love that I couldn't get from him. I started liking boys. I started talking to boys. This was the beginning of making a million mistakes and some that cost me many years of misery. See, what my dad did to me at the young age of 9 years old was make me feel like I wasn't important. So, any boy that could make me feel important, made me feel good. I was looking for a replacement for a dad at a very early age. Not knowing this is what I was doing at this time because I was too young. I was missing something and trying to fill a void. I didn't know that this would cause issues throughout my entire life but this caused me so many years of pain. So many years of bad decision making. The main reason is that I didn't have an example in front of me to show me the way.

I did call my dad back that same day when I calmed down to ask him why he wouldn't tell me the truth and better yet, why he would take two children if he cannot take all. He responded that it was really expensive to fly us all to him and therefore he couldn't afford it. From that day forward, I felt disconnected from him. It was a turning point for me and I felt alone. I felt unimportant and there was nothing my mom or anyone could do. Even asking her husband of that time to represent me and be a father figure to me wasn't good enough. Although my mom husband did agree to the task, it wasn't good enough because he was not my real dad. He was someone else's dad and not even 3 years later, my mom divorced him for his infidelity and he was no longer my step-father.

So now here I was 10 years old, my father was absent in the home and now I have gone through two stepfathers. My mom was doing the absolute best she can do but unfortunately, she continued to choose the wrong man. It wasn't any fault of hers because she was lost and she didn't even expect to divorce my father but she had no choice due to infidelity in their relationship. Hanging on in there we moved yet once again. But this time mom found a house very close to the house we were in with my old step-father so that we didn't have to change schools and keep starting over. We literally moved 4 blocks away and I truly appreciated staying at my school.

Change

My mom started dating again and this time she found this really cool guy named Andrew. Andrew was really handsome and one of the funniest men she ever dated. They seemed to be getting along good and he had two daughters which made me happy because now I had sisters that I could bond with. Considering my mom had two boys and one girl I really wanted sisters. Unfortunately, his daughters lived in Texas with their mom but they visited with us frequently and it felt like they were always around. I built a strong bond with them and I really loved having them around. One was my age and the other was younger by about 5 years old when we met but it didn't matter to me. It was a way for me to have something new and fun. As time passed, Andrew and my mom got close and we moved to a new home all together. I actually say my mom happy for once. She was really happy and things started to get better.

My new stepdad bought me my very first bike and showed me how to ride it. I loved him and he was nice to both my brothers. We were a real family for the first time and I was thrilled. My mom was still working hard and her husband was too so, I spent many hours home alone. What my mother was trying to do at this time was to create her own insurance company and get her own office. I was very proud of her for this step and it made her very profitable, but it was also very time-consuming. To the point where she was never home and I was literally raising myself. My oldest brother was off to college and my middle brother was always in the streets or with friends until he too left for college. It left me alone because my stepfather worked over an hour away and so I began to wander in the wrong direction.

Us moving to a new home made me transfer from my school with all my friends at the end of my 7th grade year. So, my mom transferred me to the school in the neighborhood which was named Southwood Middle School. I walked to and from school every day. The walk was not very short either it was about a fifteen minute to twenty minute walk each way. I had my own set of keys to let myself in and I studied, did my homework, and often cooked my own dinner because my mom had to work to provide a roof over our head. Her husband was also working and his parents owned a liquor store off 119th and Halsted and he would often stop to see them on his way home. So, by the time anyone came home most times I was sound asleep or watching television. I stayed on the phone all day and night with my friends particularly my cousin Sweetie. She was who I considered my partner in crime. We did everything together and she also was suffering because she was losing her father to lung cancer. So, when I got transferred my 8th grade year to Southwood Middle School I was with Sweetie all the time. I didn't know anyone else.

I joined the cheerleading team and I was excited to meet new friends. But for some reason, I kept getting into fights and getting suspended from school. My mom would come to get me, get my hair done, and then when it was time to go back to school, I was cuter than the day I left. My mom tried to keep me cute with all the nicest clothes and she got my hair done faithfully every other week. I think it was her way to ensure I knew she was taking care of things for me by ensuring I was groomed. I appreciated it because soon enough, I was known in school as the girl who always changes her hair and always get her hair done. This was something good to be known by because soon after I met a young boy named Jay and he became my best friend. He later became my boyfriend and the crazy part about it was no one knew what I was doing because my mom nor my stepdad was ever home. My mom got me my own phone line put in my room and that was probably the biggest mistake she could have ever made.

I always acted like I was on the phone with Sweetie and 9/10 times I was, but I began talking on the phone with Jay. Jay was the basketball star at Southwood Middle School. He was a really cute, in shape, and sweet young man. His parents owned a church and his father was the pastor. He was always at church if he wasn't playing basketball. What was amazing about him was I would meet up with him when his practice was over. He could contact me at any time and I would walk out of my house to go and meet up with him halfway just to kiss him. These was some of the sweetest memories I have with any guy because he never pressured me to do anything. He would come to the school daily with gifts for me such as candy and roses. He always wrote me cute notes, walked me to my classes, and would put his jacket on me when we were away at games as

I was a cheerleader. I used to make the cheerleaders repeat cheers with his name in it and they follow suit. This was puppy love at its finest. Throughout the year, we got closer. Jay showed me attention that I was missing from childhood and even though there was nothing much he could do at such a young age, he was an ear to listen. He listened to me about my life and my complaints. He let everyone at the school know that we were an item. He was proud to claim me. We went to our 8th grade dance together in a stretch Rolls Royce and went downtown and walked around with 2 other couples of that time.

That was a time to remember and I will never forget how I felt that night. I was cold in my dress and he gave me his jacket and on our way home from the dance, he wrapped his arms around me hugging and kissing on me. I know I was only 14 years old but, I found love. Days after, we had a half of day and I traveled with a group of kids to his house and that was the day I lost my virginity. We didn't plan to do this and we were all just hanging out. But, we end up traveling to his sister's room and we were kissing and hugging again and it just kind of happen. He was gentle with me but it wasn't what I thought it would be. It hurt and I wasn't advised this was how it would feel. I just wanted him to have it because I loved him. So, we both lost our virginity that day and it was a very sweet moment.

When I got home I found myself bleeding and I didn't understand why. It was crazy because I lost my virginity before I even got my first period. Apparently, Jay popped my cherry and it is very normal for a young girl to have bleeding after engaging in sex for the first time. I was scared but I had no one to talk to about it. I didn't even tell him. I kept it to myself, put on one of my mother's sanitary napkins, and moved on. Jay and I kept this our secret and we told no one. Not a friend, not our siblings, or our parents. I was happy that he didn't brag or share our personal situation with anyone. At that age, young boys love to discuss what they did or what they got done to other friends to gain cool points or bragging rights. But, not for Jay and he was very mature past his age group. He said nothing. Upon time for graduation, I was saddened because we knew that due to our address we would not attend the same school and on top of that his parents moved him to Indiana. When we parted ways, I never heard from him and we were sad to separate from each other.

Disappointment

When I began high school at my new school away from Jay, I was all alone again but I did have my cousin Sweetie with me. I met this guy named Devon the summer before high school and we became really cool. His brother was dating my cousin Sweetie and so I saw them a lot. Devon began liking me and he was a sophomore while I was a freshman. I was telling him that I had a boyfriend named Jay but I hadn't heard from him and I guess we were no longer together. Devon asked me to be his girlfriend and I agreed. Life started picking up again and we were hanging out going to Great America and dressing alike. Devon also played basketball and his family was an amazing family. His mom was cool and his dad was funny, so I fit right in.

Like always I was alone at home so I started ditching school with Devon. I got away with it for a very long time. It even got to the point where I would have him spend the night at my mom's house or I would spend the night at his. We were enjoying our time until we got caught one day by my older brother Leroy. He went to look for me at school and I was not there. He immediately called my mother and she contacted the police, and they found me at Devon's house. I was grounded forever my mom said, but again she had to work so I would leave and go see him anyway many times a week. It was all fun and games until I got pregnant at 15 and didn't know.

I finally got my first menstrual cycle at age 15 and right after my first period, I was pregnant. When I got it, I wasn't scared or worried. I told my mom and she went to get me my proper care items. I didn't know I was pregnant because I kept getting my cycle month after month. Until one day I was sitting in a woodshop class with Devon and an elbow ran across my stomach and he saw it. I was like hold up what was that! Devon jumped out of his seat with fear and walked away from me. I had no clue what to do, but we knew then that there was a baby in there and we were scared. All this ditching school, having sex when we weren't supposed to, finally caught up to me.

I was scared to approach my mom but when she came home late the next day, I went into her room and just started crying to tell her that I wasn't a virgin any longer and she immediately asked me when my last period. I told her I didn't know even though I did. She did not go to work the next day at all and she took me to Planned Parenthood to get an abortion. When I got to the clinic they were preparing to give me a test and to tell me how far along I was. They told my mom that I was probably about 3 months pregnant, but the only way to be sure is to give me a blood test. When they started testing me and giving me all these examinations, we were shocked by our results. I was 7 months and 1 week pregnant, I was dilated 1cm, and I was told to go right to a hospital. My mother was distraught and I was crying. I felt like a failure and that although I was a straight A-student, I disappointed my mom but more importantly myself.

My mom worked really hard to provide for us all and I knew she was hurt. She immediately put me on punishment for the rest of the year so she said. She took me to the hospital to stop my labor and the hospital gave me prenatal care and steroids because they said that I was way too small. My baby went the entire pregnancy without any prenatal care and therefore I needed to get some immediately. Once the labor was stopped, my mom wanted to meet with Devon and his mom and then my granny and my aunt to discuss our plan.

I felt really embarrassed to tell my granny and I felt awful that I did this to myself and my family. I didn't know what to do and soon after everyone at high school knew I was pregnant. My dance team kicked me off and I wasn't allowed to participate in prom elections so I couldn't even get nominated for prom queen. I met with my counselor and she told me that she knew I was a very smart young lady and that if I wanted she could help me out and allow me to skip a grade as long as I agreed to take classes at night at American School. I agreed so that I didn't have 2 more years of high school to complete instead of one.

The baby was born 10 weeks later, I was supposed to be a junior in high school but instead, I was a senior in high school. I was finally 16 years old. Although a lot was going on throughout that time, I did not talk to my dad, nor did he know I was pregnant or even birthed a child. He found out through his insurance bills. He was looking at his bills one day and saw a lot of gynecologist charges and labor and delivery charges and called my mom. Now my parents barely spoke so my mom might have forgotten to tell him because we were pressed for time to get a nursery together, a baby shower, and change our whole house around to prepare for the baby girl I was delivering.

My dad called and straight asked my mom, "Is our daughter having a baby"? My mom didn't know what to say but, "um yea". My mom was also embarrassed because it felt like she failed as well as a parent. I wasn't a fast girl either, I was looking for a relationship just way too early. I wasn't talking to a lot of boys, just one. This was a turnaround for my dad. He was very upset to find out he was a grandfather at a young age. My dad flew into town the very next day to meet his granddaughter and to see me. I was happy and scared at the same time to see him. But, most importantly, I was glad that he would make me a priority and come into town in such an urgency. For the first time in my life, I felt important to him and I kind of liked the attention I received. He came into town with clothes for my new baby who

I named Daisy. Daisy looked just like me and she was the most beautiful thing I have ever seen. She was a very calm baby. She was a jewel. I am grateful and was grateful to be her mother.

Devon and I graduated together and decided to go off to college together. We attended Jackson State University together in Jackson, Mississippi. Everything was going pretty good up until one day his brother got into a bad fight and one of my best friends called his phone. We just got new prime mobile phones and received new numbers. So, I was quite shocked she had his number. We only had the numbers for two days. When she broke the news to him he was quite upset. I would have been too because it was his little brother. Although I love his little brother I was more upset she had his number. Sadly, I had an intuition and I was right. They were actually sleeping together behind my back. I broke up with my child's father and transferred schools to go back to Illinois. I was hurt, sad, and confused. But, I had to be strong to raise our daughter and I moved on. I never got back with him and we never messed around ever again. We were done. That was the day, I felt good about not being a doormat even though we were very young. I would feel bad about it from time to time but, not enough to get back with him.

Pain

For the first time in my life, I was single. I was alone however, it didn't bother me because I was used to being alone all while growing up. But, I was heartbroken and confused. I called my dad when we broke up to tell him. I was looking for some support. He wasn't exactly sympathetic and his response was quite heartbreaking. He told me that I was acting like Devon was going to be there with me the entire time Daisy was young and be better than him. He wanted to make a point to me that Devon did the same thing as him to make a point. His point actually hurt my feelings. Although his words were truthful and hurtful, he did offer me some financial assistance monthly to help me out during my single motherhood. It was needed and greatly appreciated.

The one thing that remains true about my dad is that he might not be present, but financially he will assist. I think that is one of his best traits to be a provider. I wanted his presence but his financial assistance was better than many fathers. He couldn't be present anyway due to him living in another state. By now I was 19, a single mother, living on my own, gave my virginity away at 13, got pregnant at 15, lost one of my closest friends, and was extremely lost, alone, and confused. I was now living in Dekalb, Illinois. I was attending Kishwaukee Community College to finish up some prerequisites.

I joined this single mother club at Northern Illinois University. This club was one that I will never forget. We met once a week and talked and networked with each other. You could bring your children and they can play during the meeting. It was a good way to meet friends and to meet people who were just like you. I met this one really cool girl and our daughters were friends. Our daughters were the same age. What was really cool about this group was that you could bring your child's too little clothes and pick up some gently used clothes. The group asked for you to wash the unwanted clothes, label the clothes by size and sex of the child, and leave it in the giveaway room. At that time Daisy just grew out of 2T. So, I got a bag, washed her clothes, labeled the bag girls (2T). Picked up a bag of girl's 3T and I was grateful. This supportive group helped me out as I was already living in subsidized apartments and had an EBT card. I had become part of the welfare system and was now a statistic.

As time went on, 9 months had passed and I was still living in Dekalb before I spoke to Devon again. Yes, I was wrong for ignoring him and his family, but I was hurt and I needed time to myself away from all the pain. At this point I felt like every man in my life was just hurting me or leaving me. So, I ran away from life and from everyone. I didn't even talk to my favorite cousin Sweetie. I went aloof and I didn't want to be bothered. I literally ignored every call from Devon's family except his father's calls. For some reason, I would always answer his calls as he always wanted to check on his granddaughter. He used to give me advice and his exact words were, "you can ignore him for right now, but don't wait too long". I always obliged and said okay. But, I didn't know how long it would take me to talk to him. I was angry.

By the 9th month of silence, I finally answered for him and allowed him to come up to the school to see Daisy. He came and stayed the night for a couple of days to spend time with her. This was probably a mistake because we kept arguing and we couldn't get along. It got so bad that I got kicked out of my apartment. I couldn't believe that they kicked me out but they did. They provided me a 30 day notice and I left to go back home with my mom and stepfather.

When I got home I began to realize my mom and my step father were having issues. My stepfather Andrew suffered from substance abuse and it caused division in their marriage. I remember one day when I was there our light bill got so high that the lights got cut off. My mom had to come up with over $1,000 just to get it cut back on plus the fees they charge on top of that. As she was trying to get it together, we were lighting candles to illuminate the house. I felt that it was really romantic and we had a fireplace so we also lit some wood. My stepfather Andrew was so upset that he left the house to go to his mom's and dad's home. He said for us to call him when the lights were cut back on. This made me not really like Andrew too much. I literally lost respect for him for a long period of time. My mom did too and they broke up immediately afterward. I started feeling bad for my mom and her repeatedly failed relationships. My mom has always had a big heart but she just kept ending up with the wrong guy.

I started looking for my own place because I was almost 20 years old and I was still in school. I was attending Chicago State University at this time. I was going to school to be a teacher. That shortly changed when I was told by a student that he doesn't listen to his mom so what makes me think he will listen to me. He was right, it wasn't enough money in being a teacher and I was just a teacher assistant at this time. So, I changed my major and changed schools. I got a townhome in Park Forest, Illinois and registered for school at Governors State University to complete my Bachelor's Degree.

Foolishness

I finally caught up with my cousin Sweetie and she introduced me to this guy named Mook. I thought Mook was the best man in the world of course. I was 19 and he was 26 and I was way over my head. I think that because he had way more money than me, I was attracted to him even more. Not knowing I was following in my mom's footsteps in selecting the wrong guy yet once again. Mook was fun and immature at the same time. But at 19 I overlooked the fact that he was immature. I did things I never did with him and I am ashamed that I allowed him to get over on me as he did.

Although I was an independent young lady and had my own car, own place, own job, and going to school I still suffered from being very foolish. I stayed with Mook for 15 years after that and I went through so much hell. At the end of that relationship, I suffered from debt, bad credit, and even divorce. I knew that from that relationship ending something just had to change. Mook had one too many chances and I should have left him after year one. From all the lies, him not coming home at night, not proposing until ten years later, to not living together for 10/15 years, to even being a drunk. I should have known better. He changed over the years and right when I thought things were getting better, things were actually getting worst. I believe the biggest issue is that I was graduating and elevating every year to better myself and he was dreaming of elevating but moving at a slower pace than I'd like. See, his dreams were fine for the average woman, but I have always been far from average. To stay with Mook, I would have had to pass up my dreams to follow his for the rest of my life. I did this for a little while and even dropped out of school for two years but as you can see it didn't pay off.

For the longest time, I allowed a man to convince me that I had to pay for love or worst, give up my dreams to be loved. I thought it was normal for your spouse to go out every Friday with friends and hangout weekly. I actually thought it was perfectly fine for your spouse to exclude you from major events. What's even worst is I thought it was okay to not have children with your spouse and give up your right to have children to fit the needs of someone else. For many years that is what I did. But, filing for divorce was one of the things that help me realize that I was starting to be just like my mom and I was on a journey to failure. I didn't realize what went wrong and what role I played in me selecting the wrong man. I was now ending my third relationship and I needed to find myself to do so.

For the next entire year after separating from Mook, I stayed alone. It felt like I was on drugs and having withdrawals.

I fought myself time after time to not go back. To not get back comfortable and get back in a one-sided situation. Mook was sending me messages and calling me and I had to block him to be able to move forward. Walking away from a 15 year relationship wasn't easy, but I could no longer be a doormat. I could no longer cry out for attention from him that I was never going to get. I could no longer pay for everything. I could no longer be used. I could no longer be married and live separately. I could no longer be disrespected. I could no longer live his way. I also could no longer be last. In Mook's life, I was last and I learned a very valuable lesson over the years and that is, if you are not first, you are last! Now I live that way and I will take that lesson with me forevermore.

One of my biggest issues was facing the embarrassment of getting a divorce. It is one of the most embarrassing moments for me besides my teenage pregnancy. I felt like I was a failure and I didn't want anyone to know about the troubles

I had in our Central Park home. But I subjected myself to being foolish for him because I thought at least I was married. But, married or unmarried, you should never want to be foolish. I was foolish by thinking it was okay to accept anything thrown my way. I remember crying myself to sleep all alone because Mook was never home. He literally lived in the streets and instead of spending time with his newlywed wife, he continued to tell me he felt like he was being penalized for being married. Being penalized meant that he was to stay in the house. Staying in the house away from all his homies that he typically would be around on Friday nights. His claim to fame was that he wasn't cheating but any man that comes home to his wife after 9am should not be shocked when they are accused of cheating. Mook didn't come home on our agreed upon time ever and therefore, for me to continue to accept that behavior made me not only foolish, but it also made me just plain dumb.

Now that I have had the time to

process and analyze what I was going through, I have no excuse but to hold myself accountable. See when you are foolish for a man rather he is your husband or not, you lose. Plain and simple and there is no coming back from that either. Once you accept one form of disrespect, you will continue to deal with disrespect. It will not stop and no man will change. They are who they are, and it is a foolish concept to believe that they will change. I stayed in my situation for a variety of reasons, but the only reason that made sense to me was that I didn't know any better. Due to my lack of experience in dating and lack of example, I was foolish. Being in that relationship made me question myself time over time again on how was I this intelligent, independent woman, yet so damn foolish. It just didn't add up for me and what's worst is that I didn't need him financially. I just wanted to beat a time clock and be married before the age of 30. That was foolish as well and it didn't make any sense to me that I could not do better.

I allowed myself to lie to my own self and believe it. I thought that I could really change a man who doesn't believe in marriage as I did. Men who are stuck in their ways are exactly that, stuck! So, when I stepped out on faith and walked away with no idea what was going to come, I was faced with the one thing I never faced before. Something that hit me like a brick in the face and I didn't know I would go through so much. Even though I had a whole plan, I couldn't hide from it. My plan was working well especially with getting an apartment, selling the homes, switching the children's schools, and even putting all of my belongings in a storage unit. Everything that I needed to have I did. Even getting a new puppy to distract the children worked out perfectly. I was thinking I outsmarted everything and my plan was error-proof. But, indeed it wasn't. Surely, since I had a roof over me and the children head, food in the refrigerator, and I had air in my lungs, I would be just fine.

There are just something that you cannot plan for and I wanted peace and quiet which is why I moved to Indiana where no one could find me or even run into me. It truly worked well, up until I finally got settled into my apartment. I haven't rented an apartment in over 17 years and I was shocked to downsize after coming from such a big brand new home that was built in 2009 with 4 bedrooms, 4 bathrooms, and a 3 car garage. I was living on top of the world in my eyes. I had multiple vehicles and my dream car of that time which was a Porsche Panamera.

What I was faced with couldn't be avoided. It was one of the biggest tasks and elements one person can deal with in one lifetime and that is to deal with yourself without any distractions, not any friends, not even a side piece. Just sit and deal with your decisions, look at your life, and reflect upon what direction you are headed in and what have you learned from this failed marriage you just exited. See, oftentimes people jump right into something else and they think the grass is greener on the other side, but it is certainly not. I wasn't ready for a new relationship or to deal with another man as I was broken, hurt, and worst, damaged goods.

I used to be this beautiful soul and I was torn down to ground zero. It was a humbling experience, yet a painful one. To think, that I thought I had it all together but I just didn't. No matter how intelligent I was, or how many degrees I earned, or even that I had a good heart helped this time. I always did people right and I always opened up my heart to the most undeserving people. I am and always will be the type to be resourceful and helpful to others, but I had been taken advantage of by the person who I thought loved me. But, growing pains let me know that there is a difference between love and in love because sitting in that apartment by myself for a year single made me learn that Mook loved me, but, he was not in love. I also learned that I loved him more than he loved me. It was foolish of me to love him so much and there was nothing I could do but move on. I dealt with myself for the first time ever and to me it was the most difficult task. I was now entering a phase called, "the storm". But, one thing I know for sure is, when a storm comes it is unexpected, unwanted, and full of surprises. However, each storm shall too pass one day.

Storm

Dealing with yourself and learning about yourself in solitude is something the average person wouldn't dare do. Part of the reason women stay in relationships that are not good for them is that they are afraid to face the storm. Listen, I did this without any alcohol, I refrained from sex, and I decided to pray every night. I asked God to heal my broken heart, help me heal from all the pain in my heart. I had so much grief and pain. The storm that I went through was one I was not prepared to deal with. It was like having drug withdrawals and I do not do drugs nor have I ever. The first couple of nights were rough.

When I first became single again, I wasn't in my apartment in Indiana. I was in my home on Central Park, the marital home. It was a quiet experience. I remember calling all my friends all on the same day and crazily they were all unavailable. It was God forcing me to deal with myself and even not calling my mom was a good idea. So, I put my phone up. I didn't watch any television, I didn't cook either, I just sat in the bed looking up to the ceiling talking to God. I sat in this bed for a good 48 hours before I got up to go to work again. I couldn't even face my job. At that time, I was too embarrassed and I couldn't stop crying. I couldn't think straight. I went to the grocery store and purchased pop tarts, cereal, milk, TV dinners, and lunchables for the children. I just wanted to be sure my children could microwave and use the toaster to eat without my assistance. Thank God I have a teenager to help with the smaller children because I was in a dark place. I was stuck and ashamed.

I didn't want to be anybody's wife, friend, daughter, sister, or even mother.

I was fully depressed, and no one could pull me out but God. I fought myself for taking such a huge stance without properly thinking about the consequences, but after trying counseling for 3 years straight and having the same issues over and over again, I knew things wouldn't change. So, I stepped out on faith and prayed for better days. I must have composed ten messages to my ex that day and deleted each and every one. I wanted to say so much but I knew nothing would change. Everything would lead back to us being together just to break up yet once again. I knew that there would be nothing to change us or him for that matter. He didn't want the things in life I wanted nor has he ever. I practically had to live with the fact that I pretty much gave a man an ultimatum after dating me for 10 years and me threatening to walk away. Just so no one else had me, he married me. That was the dumbest shit I could have ever done. But in reality, it was actually foolish on both ends.

Part of my storm was actually fasting. I decided to give up meat for 90 days and I end up losing 16 lbs. I drank green smoothies and detoxed not only my life but my body too. I was eating raw fruits and vegetables only with maybe a boiled egg or two for dinner. I lost my appetite and I stopped caring about how I looked. Anybody that knows me knows that I care too much about my appearance and that I had to be depressed if I stopped caring. I didn't comb my hair, I kept on a scarf. I wore big t-shirts and jogging pants. I didn't shop, spend much money because I had to pay the mortgage alone for two homes. One of my rental homes I was trying to sell so I didn't have a tenant.

I was paying for two light bills, two gas bills, two water bills, and then catching up on all things that were left behind. I know now that it was finally over because the one thing about me is if I have to take care of everything alone, I will prefer to be alone. There is nothing worse than having a man who is present but couldn't or should I say, wouldn't do anything. There is no point to be with a man who didn't want to be a provider and the fact that my own father supported us financially showed me better. So, the point behind this storm was almost to punish myself for being foolish. To punish myself until I find my own value and self-worth.

I was still finding items that were left behind and were packing them while I clean out the house for sale as well. Packing kept me busy but every time I found something, it broke me down. I am not a big cry baby and therefore I was surprised to see tears come down my face. Since my childhood disappointments, I wasn't easily moved. But this storm hit me differently. It was a huge change and alteration to my life. It was an unexpected life change that only God could get me out of at this moment. As I prayed day in and day out, nothing seemed to change. Well, at least it appeared that way. But, I do believe that God will teach you things on his timing and definitely not yours. So, I toughed this storm out and just had to face myself and deal with my poor decisions.

I also expected to hear from his family and yet they didn't call. I expected to really hear from his children because I helped raise them for 15 years, but they never called. I guess once I stopped doing all that I was doing and buying, I was no longer useful or they no longer cared. I know that it was common for everyone to stand by his side, but I didn't think it would go like that. Finally, I received a call from his dad to say hello and check on me and the girls. He was my favorite person in their family besides his mom. So, I wasn't surprised that it was him to break the silence. I always loved his parents and I knew that this would be difficult for me.

Every day that went by made me stronger but every memory in that house made me weaker. This is why I end up getting an apartment and just leaving the house vacant until sold. I couldn't stand to be in that house any longer. I didn't want to remember anything because although there might have been some good memories, there was a hell of a lot more bad memories. Memories that were hitting me hard and hindering me from moving on. The children were feeling my pain as well because his family never called to even check on them not one time; just one call from his dad.

I was starting to think about how could this be, but it was my new truth. It was my new life and it was what I thought I needed. Even if I didn't think I needed it, I had no choice but to deal with it and weather this storm. I wasn't going to play with anyone heart and even though I feel as though mine was played with, it wouldn't be right to do the same. As the old saying goes, two wrongs don't make a right. So, to contact him or to act a certain way when my heart was telling me that I was no longer in love, wasn't mentally healthy. So, I didn't and I am glad I didn't do this to him.

I began working out and finally

going outside of the home during my alone time. It was just to walk around a track or to let the girls play at the park. I found myself in a mad stage. I was mad as hell for a really long time. I was madder at myself more than anything. Not only was I throwing pictures off the walls, I was also throwing pictures away. Wedding pictures, family pictures, and any picture with him in it, I tossed in the garbage. I went through my cell phone and deleted every picture of us in it. I logged on to my social media and deleted any post with his name or photo. I didn't want to be reminded of a failed marriage nor him. I had full rage and all I could see was red. I had never been this mad before in my entire life. I was shocked I let myself get this low. I was now mailing things to his mother's home instead of allowing him to grab them when I wasn't home. Then, one day while going to check the mail, I got some tickets in the mail that he got in my name. I finally broke my silence and reached out to him via text to pay the

$500 in fees he received in my name. Wishful thinking because he still hasn't paid that. I would have included it in the divorce, but he wouldn't have paid and I would still be married.

I was disappointed in my choices in my relationships. All of them since the beginning of me dating was a failure. I was so angry at this time in my choices in men. I couldn't seem to grasp how and why this was all happening to me. There was no logical explanation. I didn't understand why I couldn't find happiness when I had so much to offer to a man. I was an amazing stepmother and an awesome wife. But, yet I keep attracting myself to the wrong man. I was starting to feel like I was following in my mother's footsteps, I did have children and they were all girls so it was pertinent to find someone who I could trust around my children. I didn't want anyone to bother them or mistreat them. Same as my mother who often married for convenience. I thought I would be different and marry due to love. But, this wasn't the case obviously for me because I began to select men off of the wrong things.

What was crazy is during my time alone, not many men tried to talk to me. I think it was because I looked a mess. Typically all types of men approach me on a daily but it is the devil and only when you are taken, are you tested. It was like God was trying to avoid me finding a temporary satisfaction to cover up the storm that I must go through. I thought about it and I did talk to a couple of guys along the way but it wasn't anything serious because I was still legally married. So, I didn't want to have it in the back of my mind that I was committing adultery. But, I did talk with God and he knew that my relationship was long overdue and it been over.

I think that when I stop fighting for my marriage, everything fell apart. I know that I was always the one willing to work things out and patch stuff up. So, I truly was seeing what he would do because there is nothing worse than a one-sided relationship. When I faced my storm I realized it truly was a one-sided relationship and it was best I moved on because I deserved for someone to love me as hard as I loved them. I also deserved to be in a relationship whereas I have someone fighting for me and wanting to be with me. I wanted someone who wouldn't want to leave my side ever and want to spend time with me instead of me fighting to get time. I needed someone who didn't make me schedule an appointment for a date. I needed someone who was all about me. I would have never gotten that in my marriage with Mook.

I was finally becoming okay with my decision. I decided I would start going out with my cousin Sweetie. Which in turn ended up another bad mistake. My cousin was in a toxic relationship and it caused her and our family many bad memories. One day I went out with her and we were hanging having a good time like we always do and she left my house at the end of the night to go home. She called me moments later and she told me that she had got into a fight. I hopped in my truck to get to her immediately and to my surprise, it was another female there and a guy. The women were fighting over this one guy. It was nothing I wanted to be a part of but unfortunately I was a part of it. When I was leaving to go back home because the fight was over, my cousin Sweetie's boyfriend drove off and totaled my truck. He hit my truck so hard my airbags deployed and I was so angry. I was angry for so many reasons. One, because my truck was paid off so, totaled meant I would have to get another one. But, crazily the car that hit me he was driving didn't have any insurance. I was sick and it was just another issue that I had to face.

The other young lady who was fighting actually gave me her telephone number and offered to pay for my truck repairs. She was younger than all of us by at least 10 years but I had so much respect for her. Her name was Ashley and she said that since it was a love triangle that she felt it was only fair that my cousin Sweetie, the boyfriend, and her split the bill and she will make payments to pay me 1/3 of the bill. I was totally shocked and I admired her for her maturity. But the sad part of this situation is that I never heard from my cousin Sweetie or her boyfriend again. This was my ride or die cousin who always was with me and it hurt me to not speak to her ever again especially over some money and a truck, but still to this day, I haven't heard from her. She and the boyfriend got back on good terms and never contacted me again.

So, now I was separated from my spouse, not speaking to any of my friends, and now into with the only person, I ever trusted with everything and who has been my favorite person besides my granny my whole life. My storm started to get worst and even lonelier. But, again I crawled up in a shell and went back in the house and never to go out again for over 6 months. I just raised the children and stayed home. My storm was a quite lonely one but it allowed me to begin processing some things.

I began a conquest to find out what was wrong with me and why was I going through what I was going through. What happened to me and what wrong turn did I make in life to get me to this point? I began analyzing my friendships and asking why am I their friend? I wanted to learn more about myself without a man present. I wanted to reach for some answers so I went to God and I began to think about the beginning of times even from my childhood to find some type of solution. So that is what I did so that I can find out how did I get to a point in my life where I became so damn independently foolish? I found my answer that I went to seek. The answer was from the beginning of my life when my father was absent.

Absence

There is a saying that states. "Absence makes the heart grows fonder". I have to admit I totally disagree with that. Absence does not make the heart grow fonder. It actually raises awareness of neglect. Due to my father not being present in the home growing up, it forced me to be lost. I didn't have an example of what type of man I should be with. There was no one teaching me my worth or my value. Here I am independent and foolish and recognizing the fact that I was independent while being raised. I also lack a good family structure, which didn't leave me any good examples.

My whole life was filled with my parents getting married, getting divorced, and remarrying. So, there was no way I could even know what a successful marriage looks like when I haven't seen one. It was easy for me to get divorced as well because it was a part of the norm and unfortunately I end up marrying someone who didn't have a good example as well. From the beginning of time, when my father engaged in infidelity and left my mom, I began being in an unfortunate situation. I often wonder would I have not gone through so much trouble if my dad was there. Growing up without him was the beginning of all the pain, the agony, and the disappointment.

I was lost growing up for the longest time. I lacked confidence, I wasn't sure of myself, I hated myself. I didn't like my teeth, my boobs were too big for me, and my legs were chicken. It took birth control to get my body proportionate and that wasn't on purpose. I had a breast reduction at age 19. I had a gap in my teeth and I got it closed at age 18. I had curly shoulder length hair but to me it was nappy. The best part of my hair was my bang because it was super full. I have always had edges thank God, but I just wasn't happy and didn't feel pretty. But how could I? Every man I was with disappointed me or cheated on me. My father was supposed to be my first love and the first man to tell me that I was pretty, but he wasn't. He was actually the first man to hurt me. By the time I learned to walk he already had another child on the way.

I was hurting growing up because of the way I had to live. My mom struggled to take care of us. She had a high school education, no college, and no trade. At that time her highest career position was the Assistant Manager at Taco Bell. That isn't enough money to take care of 3 children of which 2 were boys. Boys could eat you out of a house and a home. Buying clothes for three growing children at age 23 and heartbroken, was tough. I watched my mom struggle through my father's absence. Any child who grows up without their father in the home will have what I had, and that was a void. I could only imagine having a household with two incomes, life would have been completely different for me.

Some of my closest friends of that time actually had their parents still together. So even having cheer or dance performances and watching my friend's fathers come in with flowers made me tear up. I never had that, and there is nothing I could do to get that. I was envious and jealous of girls with dads. The point of even discussing this is to clearly prove that a father's absence makes a world of difference. There are more than 19.7 million children annually who live in a home without their father present (US Census Bureau, 2020). That statistic bothers me to know many children who live a life just like me and there are many more children who will live without their father present in the home and it breaks my heart. I wish I could hug them all, but unfortunately but I cannot.

There is another old saying that states that when your father leaves your momma that doesn't mean he leaves you! That is nothing further from the truth because they leave you too. Once the father leaves that home he is gone forever and then he becomes the visitation dad instead of raising you daily. What I wanted was to be raised by my father daily. I deserved that and so did my brothers. My middle brother suffered more than I did from our father's absence and although later in life I was able to move forward, I still believe to this day, he cannot. One of my biggest issues was that my dad got married right away and my mom was sad the majority of my life growing up. So, to know he fell in love with someone else and their marriage also failed, made me feel like he changed my life for nothing. Now I do believe that everything happens for a reason, and I wasn't old enough to understand the rationale behind my parent's separation, however, the aftereffects hit me like a ton of bricks.

My entire life I always had this absent void in my heart. I wanted to be loved by a man. So, part of not having a good example set for me during my childhood is the reason why I chose the wrong men. I didn't know what type of man I should have. I didn't know what qualities he should possess. Most little girls want a man just like their dad. I couldn't honestly say that when I was growing up. What is crazy is I have always been a daddy's girl, so I think my father's absence in the home really took a toll on my life, and my ability to make decisions. I will never forget when I lost my virginity and I felt alone afterward because the boy who took it and I was no longer together. I cried and cried saying I wanted my dad. But I knew that he wouldn't be there, nor was we close enough to tell him. See, what my father didn't know then and I am sure he knows now, is that I needed him to protect me. Protect me from the wrong boys and/or men taking advantage of me. Now I gave my virginity away because I thought I was in love and although I was not forced, I shouldn't have been engaging in sexual activity at 13. But, I fell in love so early because I didn't have that type of love at home. I was missing it and Jay, the boy who took my virginity, gave me what I was missing. So I gave my virginity to him at only 13 years old.

Jay knows how it feels to be raised with both parents because his parents are still together. It made him a better person and he heavily values marriage. He was every bit of respectful, gentle, and kind to me during our childhood. My point is he has a living example of how a successful relationship looks like and he got to see how to make it last. I was the one who had no clue. I attached myself to him at an early age because it was the first taste of pure love I ever had. I hate to blame my father for such a big mishap in my life because I love my dad, and I know he is a great man. But, at that time, my father's career and military rankings were more important. He valued them more than family and because he did, I grew up with a void.

When I broke up with Daisy's father,

I also felt a void and it was another moment when I wanted to reach out to my dad. Actually, that time I did but my father wasn't very supportive of that relationship, so he wasn't very sympathetic. He kept reminding me of how I told him that my child's father would be around for Daisy. Crazily that statement is still true today. Daisy's father is a good dad for her and he is around and always has been. So, I didn't lie to my dad, but my dad can be the type to hold grudges and he also will throw in your face where you went wrong. He has to give his two cents on every situation no matter what mental state you are in. You have to be prepared to hear I told you so or I knew that wouldn't work. He is just an old school dad and this is how he was raised, so he can't help himself. My dad wants everyone to learn a lesson for their actions. I am used to it now, but when I was younger it definitely bothered me and it made me not talk to him as much as I'd like.

The absence I felt in my former

marriage was a whole other level. I felt like I was in a marriage all by myself and there was nothing I could do, but leave. My ex-husband was the type of man who was absent at my family functions, parties my friends were hosting, and even some important milestones, and functions. He just didn't want to go anywhere unless it was with his family, and if you got him to do anything, you were lucky, and trust me he reminded you. I didn't like the way he made me feel about him being a part of the family. It was something that I knew was wrong, but I decided to do what most women do and that is settle. I settled to just have someone fill a void that was left behind by my father. All my life I was chasing this absent void filler and it caused me so much pain and I truly wish that I found another hobby to help me get through it all. But, instead, I wasted 20 years of my life running behind the wrong men. I know that it was all a life lesson but I wish it didn't take away my entire youth.

I lost many years in this last relationship that I cannot simply take back.

The absence I felt when I was graduating with my Ph.D. which was my biggest accomplishment, let me further know I made the best decision. But here I was supposed to be at the happiest part of my life and I even dedicated my dissertation to him, to wake up on graduation day without him. Now, I did uninvite him to my graduation because we were no longer living together and we were no longer together. But a few weeks before my graduation ceremony he told me that he thought my degree was nothing but a piece of paper. So, I knew then that he shouldn't be there and that I needed to just leave him alone. After thinking about why we really broke up I realized it was his alcoholism that didn't allow him to make better choices within our relationship. So, on the morning of my graduation I had conflicting feelings. I had 23 family and friends attend to support me but because I was still legally married, I walked across that stage with that man's last name. I was disgusted that I graduated with his name because he didn't deserve me and I knew what we once had was over. Now, my dissertation will always have his last name on it, but I contacted my school and got a new degree printed up. I tore that degree with his last name into little bitty pieces.

Even though I was able to change his last name off of my degree I still felt his absence in my spirit. I didn't cry this time though. I just held my head up high and went on to celebrate. See one thing that men do when they envy you or not happy for you is to take away moments that are most important to you. For my ex-husband he tried to steal my joy at my Bachelor's degree graduation, my Master's degree graduation, and last, my Ph.D. graduation. His biggest issue was that I was elevating and he wasn't unfortunately. Not how he liked it. So, I had to pick myself up from that and move on and along even if I didn't want to. I will never forget the void I had that morning but for my three girls, I kept my head up high and I continued on with my day and my vacation thereafter. By the time of my graduation, I had begun feeling quite normal and used to being without him. Crazily my graduation was in January and the very next month was my birthday. This would be the very first birthday without him and it was a tough one.

His absence on my birthday was even more difficult. My friend Mikka threw me a party and all my friends came out to celebrate with me. I had a ball that night and everyone was having a good time. I shocked everyone because I cut all my hair off which is also another sign of depression. I was depressed for sure and I was dealing with it the best way I can. The young lady who I met during my car accident named Ashley even came to celebrate with me. We built a little sister bond and it's a little part of me that loves that girl. She is so sweet and so honest. She is really pretty too.

As I continued to assess my life and

how the absence of many affected me, I had no choice but to deal with a situation that I have kept hidden from the world. This situation is one of the biggest kept secrets and no one knows about me. In my life, I have suffered from absences and choosing the wrong man. But I also suffered from relationships with family members. One of my toughest challenges is dealing with my own brother. I have a brother named Leroy who is three years older than me. Most of everyone knows him because we went to high school together. Well, he and I do not speak to each other and it has caused so much confusion in my life, and even in my marriage. It is definitely part of the reason why we didn't work out. Well, my brother hurt me tremendously and for some reason, I have been able to heal from everything, but this one.

Leroy and I have always had this love-hate relationship. But he has had some terrible problems growing up. We share the same mother and father, but for some reason, we are like oil and water and just don't mix. Now I will always love my brother but for some reason, we cannot get on the same page. I have tried to be there for him and I have made some serious sacrifices in my life that even cost me my marriage at one point. But nothing matters that I did because Leroy suffered from substance abuse and he drinks a lot. Our relationship causes me so much pain and disappointment. I can't even put it in words. But for the last 9 years, we haven't spoken to each other more than a handful of times and they were all telephone transactions. Mostly because he is on the phone with my mom and she makes me speak to him. Sometimes I am the first to speak and sometimes I am not.

Our situation is very complicated and there is a lot of hurt and pain behind our past. There is going to have to be some type of Iyanla fix my life to fix the void and absence he has put in my heart. There was a point in our life where we were cool and I tried to help him get himself together but he continues to make bad choices and he has lost my trust. Leroy has fathered 5 children who are all girls. Of his five children, two of them are twins that were born in Massachusetts by a woman who also suffers from substance abuse. The twins that were born were born early only 24 weeks gestation because of the substance abuse between the two of them. These poor unfortunately twins were my nieces and at one point in time were taken into custody by DCFS due to neglect until I stepped up and took them on and adopted them. Yes, I am an adoptive mother! Surprise!

Adoption

Many people wouldn't know that I adopted the twins because when I first went through with the adoption, I was on an 8-year hiatus from all social media. Therefore, I didn't have anything to post. I feel that my story behind the twins is a very sensitive topic but it is a full part of what made me the woman I am today. The story behind the twins in one life-altering so here it is.

Leroy was married to a lady named Jada and they had two children together which are my nieces. They decided to move to Massachusetts for a better life together. Upon getting there they were working. They hired a baby sitter to watch their two children. The baby sitter was the girlfriend of Jada's cousin. Her name was Bianca. Bianca and

Leroy messed around and Bianca ended up getting pregnant. Bianca was a full Puerto Rican woman who suffers from substance abuse. Bianca had 4 children already. When she found out she was pregnant, she didn't stop using. This caused significant damage which caused her to have her twin children early. She went into labor at 24 weeks gestation and delivered the twins weighing only 1lb, 8oz a piece. They had had to stay in ICU for 87 days. Also, this is not her first set of twins. She has another set and doesn't have custody of any of her children. She now is a mother of 6 children and all 6 are in the care of others.

At the end of their time in the hospital stay, neither Leroy nor Bianca was there. They tried to contact both parents as they wanted to discuss the children's health and their care plan. No one came so they sent the twins home in a medical foster home. The medical foster home was necessary because they both needed oxygen tanks because their lungs were underdeveloped. They had severe asthma and stomach concerns. The main problem was that they were underdeveloped. By the time Leroy did go to the hospital when they were firstborn. He went and signed the birth certificate and get a copy of it. When he left the hospital he went back to Illinois to live. He was now separated from his wife because of his infidelity and bringing not one, but two children in outside of his marriage.

Once the twins went to foster care, they had extreme needs, and the foster care family that they were placed felt as though it was too much work, so they moved them to a second home, then a third home, until they reached a fourth home. The fourth home was a very nice family and the lady who had them owned a daycare. She fell in love with the twins and began adoption proceedings. DCFS took the biological mother to court and terminated her rights immediately as she didn't show up for court. After that, they reached out to Leroy. Leroy began to say he wanted custody. All of the family got together to get him things to get the children. Since I had a close friend, Cara, who had older twins, I also helped by providing her twin hand me downs. I gave him car seats and cribs.

The state of Massachusetts denied Leroy for custody due to his many addresses at first. They didn't feel as though he was responsible because he moved every year for the last 5 years. Then when it came to employment he continued to tell them lies about his job that prevented him from getting the twin girls. He kept telling them he had his own business and was the CEO of an entertainment company. Well, this is the time that his rap dream couldn't save him and didn't work. At this time, I was 26 years old and I owned my own home for about 5 years and I worked at the same place for 5 years. So, when I was approached about temporarily fostering for the twins, I had no reservations about helping my brother out. As I was his last resort before the twins became permanently adopted and he never sees them again. Anyone who knows me knows that I would do anything for my nieces and nephews. They were like my own children and I have always been the auntie of the year with all of them because I spoil them all. I love them all and I am always the fun aunt.

The twins were about 7 months old when I agreed to the everlasting task. It took 3 months to get the entire process completed. I went to training, foster mom classes, got my foster care license with the state of Illinois, and then I got approved for temporary custody. The judge told me the only condition I had was that I needed to visit them in Massachusetts to spend time with them so that they could get to know me. So, I continued to fly into Connecticut, rent a car and drive to Holyoke, Massachusetts where they were born, and visit with them during supervised visits. Each trip cost me $1,000 and I went about 4 times down there. This caused a strain on me financially so I reached out to my dad who agreed that we would split the cost.

So, my dad booked my tickets and I paid for the car. Then I paid for the tickets and he booked the car. Teamwork is what made this happen and I appreciate my dad for this. At 10 months, I was able to actually pick them up and bring them back to Illinois. In the meantime, the judge told me that I had to set up a visitation with my brother with the state with a state supervisor.

I reached out to the caseworker when I got in Illinois to set up visitation with Leroy and I told her that she didn't need to tag alone during his weekly visits as it was my brother. That decision in itself was a mistake because, after the 2nd visit, Leroy started canceling and being extremely late holding up my entire day. I began to get livid that he was too relaxed as I was only 26 and he was 29, and I only had one child and that was Daisy and she was now 9 years old. Daisy also had to get adjusted by sharing her mother as she was the only child. But during the visits, Leroy and I started arguing and getting into arguments over and over again. The twins had a really hard time getting adjusted. This was probably due to them jumping around from home to home at such an early age. Here I was, in over my head with two babies who could not walk, who have severe medical concerns, and I was a single mother. I was arguing with my brother because he wanted to remind me that he is their father and I wasn't their biological mother, and I needed to do exactly as he says.

Part of me was listening to every word until one day one of the twins started calling me momma. Leroy snapped so hard saying he doesn't wish for his children to call me anything but auntie and I was every B-word in the book. Leroy was very disrespectful towards me and I was having trouble dealing with him weekly. The reason why the twins began calling me mom was because I had a 9 year old calling me mom, and I wasn't going to mistreat them and make them call me auntie. For what? They were young and they already been through enough and I didn't feel it was necessary. By the 3rd month, the state of Massachusetts terminated Leroy's rights and banned any and all visitation. I didn't understand why. I would get weekly visits by my caseworker and she gave me the documentation showing that he had a very bad background and assault was on it therefore he is considered dangerous. I didn't understand so I started sneaking visits at his apartment. I allowed him to visit with the twins for a few hours while I run errands. I told him he cannot take them anywhere because if he got pulled over and they were with him, they told me I would have a child endangerment charge.

For the last 5 years, I also worked for the Department of Children and Family Services in their head start division and there was no way I could dare mess up what I worked so hard for. One day, I dropped the twins off for a couple of hours. When I was done with errands, I contacted Leroy to let him know I was on my way to get the girls and he was not at home. He decided to take them to Chuck E. Cheese and of course that was nice. But, the instructions to protect me were not to take them anywhere. When I explained this to him, he cursed me out and told me that these are his children and that he will do whatever the hell he wants with his children. Now the fire in me wanted to curse him out but I knew I had to get the girls back from him. So, my response was you know what, you're right, what was I thinking. Just call me when you get back, my bad. When he finally called me 3 hours later, I came to get them and when I picked up one of the twins he snatched her back from me and said he wanted to say bye. I let him have his way because it was clear that it wasn't safe for me and he was drunk.

When I drove off, I was glad to have them in my possession but I knew then I was done sneaking around from the state because I knew he would cost me my career and then my biological child Daisy and I would need a place to live messing around with him. I prayed and thanked God for returning them back to me safely. But it was my fault for not following the rules and regulations. They were set for a reason but I was so pissed, I had to call Leroy back because he totally rubbed me the wrong way and I couldn't express how I felt until I drove off and so I did. When I called him I snapped at him so bad. How dare he talked to me like that when I was doing him a huge favor. I mean this wasn't no can I borrow some sugar or do you have a couple of dollars I could borrow. This was an everyday commitment. By the time I was ready to have their 1st birthday party I didn't even want him to come. I invited him and crazily he decided it was best to take their toys and half of their gifts that people gave them to his house. Like yea, I am going to keep this and that. He was feeling really entitled. I am like why do you keep taking everything when they live with me? He kept saying these are my kid's damnit. By this time, I was fed up with his shenanigans and his ignorant tone. This was the day I just cut him off because at this point he was too difficult to deal with and if he wanted to be the father they needed, he should have done whatever he needed to do to gain custody.

I contacted the state to ask again why was his rights terminated again and the caseworker told me his rights were terminated because Leroy went to the hospital when the children were born to get a birth certificate and even filed to get a social security card but failed to come to get his children from the hospital. I knew that it had to be more than just an assault charge on his background that I found out came from him jumping on his wife Jada. They also told me that Leroy filed the twins on his taxes that same year. Now, I wasn't going to file them because their previous foster mom had them the majority of that year. Since I got them at 10 months in my home that would mean that I only had those two months out of 12 and that is against the law. But, Leroy didn't care. I called him to ask why did he file them and he said because they are his kids. I told him well next year I am filing them and I am not playing so you are not allowed to file them. To my surprise as soon as tax season came about, he filed them yet once again. I was livid and pissed.

Now let me explain why I was so pissed. I was feeding, and raising my brother's twins for over a year and a half and he did not offer me one dollar. Still to this day he has never paid me a damn thing. He knew that my salary was over the limits for welfare so he also filed to obtain food stamps in Illinois. He was receiving $733 a month also in social security for years. But he didn't give me anything for them at all. Not one thing! When the state reached out to me getting closer to their 2nd birthday they told me that I needed to make a decision. They said that the twins were getting older and needed to secure a permanent home and unless I am adopting the twins, I needed to send them back so that they get permanent placement. So, I had a decision to make. I was now 27 and in an 8-year relationship with Mook whose advice was to send them back to the state because it is too much. But, I couldn't follow his directions because I was living alone and unmarried at the time. So, I couldn't make a married decision, while single. I think that it was the only time I made a decision that wasn't foolish.

However, I end up listening to him and packed up all their belongings. I got to the airport to get on the plane to return them back to Massachusetts and I broke completely down. I broke down to the point of no return. Here I was in the middle of O'Hare Airport in Chicago with suitcases of clothes and medicine because they were extremely sickly children and I couldn't send them back to foster care to continue to get bounced around. I was the 5th house for them and I was really attached to them. They kept saying mama the whole ride to the airport and I wore sunglasses to cover my face. I was listening to a man who didn't even want to marry me after 8 years. I called the caseworker in Massachusetts and she flew to Chicago. I sat at that airport for almost 8 hours. I was stuck and she purchased a ticket and came right to me. I needed her support and I am so glad she came to me. She was like let me help you unpack their clothes and go on and take the children home. You love them and now you need to accept the fact that you are their mother. So, this is what I did. When I returned home and started unpacking, I called Mook and told him that I couldn't do it. I broke up with him and told him that we couldn't be together anymore because I loved the girls and that I couldn't dare choose him over them and I lived by myself.

Upon the departure of the caseworker I decided that I would proceed with the adoption. I told her that day, that at first I was caring for the girls for my brother sake and now I am caring for the girls for their sake. That I was all they had in life and I couldn't do it. I wouldn't be able to live with myself knowing that I did something like that. When I told Leroy that I could consider an open adoption, he told me to send them back to the state. I was very shocked at his response. I did ask him why would he say something so stupid and he told me that he would prefer for them to be anywhere in the world than with me. That day changed me forever and it ended my relationship as his sister. I know that I will always be his sister by blood but he was not the brother I knew that I grew up with. I told him that I am adopting them and he threatened my life telling me that I will come up missing, and he cannot wait until I was six feet under. Those was some harsh and hurtful words. He must have called me a million B words but I ended the call. When he told me he wishes I was dead I was done with him.

The very next day, I received a call from DCFS saying that Leroy called them to tell them not to let me have them and then he made false claims that I leave them home alone with my now 10 year old daughter Daisy. Now, this is where he took it too far. He was trying to get Daisy taken away from me. It was one thing to not want your own children with me but please don't mess with mine. I had to call Devon, Daisy's father to let him know that DCFS might contact him about these false accusations and they might want to ask him a few questions. Devon was very upset and instructed me to keep Leroy far away from his daughter and I had no choice but to respect it. Devon's wishes were followed because I didn't know what Leroy was capable of and I didn't want to find out the hard way and it ends fatally. I know this might seem a bit farfetched, but I have buried friends who didn't think it would happen to them so I stayed far away because I wanted to live for Daisy. She also needed her mother and I wouldn't be able to live with myself if I changed her life trying to help out an ungrateful man. As time went on, I was receiving mail in the twin's name. They started having phone bills in their name and all types of things. So, I asked the court when I complete my adoption can I change their names. The judge agreed plus they had very Hispanic names. They were born Isabel Guadalupe and Helena Guadalupe.

I renamed them to give them a fresh start and I felt like a new mother and I had to just take in my single mother role. I named them Chloe Isabel and Casey Helena and gave them my last name. I kept their first original names as their middle names to keep a little of their origin and help with later explaining to them their life stories. When adoption day came, I was feeling so warm and fuzzy. They were 3 when I finalized the adoption and the judge was so pleased and happy with their story that he purchased our tickets. Before arriving they asked if I had any request. I had one request for them to fulfill and they did it for me. I asked that the biological maternal family get a visit to be able to take photos so that if they ever want to know what their biological mother looked like one day, I could definitely show them and they not be wondering who she is and what she looks like. The court agreed and I was able to allow the twins to meet their biological grandmother, mother, and siblings as she had 4 other children before them that she doesn't have custody.

When we met up with her with a supervised visit in the courtroom she looked really sick. I can tell she was still using. She kept trying to explain to these two 3 year olds that she was their mother and they kept telling her that I was their mother. It really hurt her feelings but I wasn't there to hurt her, I was there to support the twins and allow them a chance to meet their biological mother in person so that I can take photos. Photos that I have stored away still to this day for when the appropriate time is right to reveal their truth. The one thing I promised is that I would tell them the truth about their life when they got older. I wanted them to know that all of their family members are the same all but me and Daisy. I was their biological aunt and Daisy is not their biological sister but their biological cousin. However, when I adopted them, I was now their legal adoptive mother and Daisy was their legal sister. We would live happily ever after together and I promised to God that I would treat them no differently than my own. They deserved everything in the world because they had an unfortunate upbringing.

What's crazy is their health was in terrible condition. In the first year, I called off 57 days to take them to different doctors' appointments. They had to see many specialists as well. They saw a behavioral specialist, a speech therapist, a pulmonary physician, a gastroenterologist, a pediatric specialist, a neurologist, and a dietician. They were so underweight that I had a special meal plan. They were behind from the drugs in their system that they had an Individualize Family Service Plan (IFSP) for children with special needs who are under 3 years old. We were doing all we could to catch them up. Their poor lungs were so underdeveloped and they took so much medicine that I would lose sleep at night with all the prescriptions that they had to take. I had an entire suitcase filled with medicine and Casey asthma was so bad she would need multiple nebulizer treatments a day.

One day during dinner I found Chloe unresponsive and having a seizure. I panicked and I didn't know what to do even though I was CPR certified with Red Cross, I didn't ever expect to have to use my training. I called 911 and they sent an ambulance. She was foaming at the mouth and I was scared. Her twin sister and Daisy were crying and scared as well. I found out that day that Chloe had epilepsy, stage 1. I contacted the state of Massachusetts and I requested history on the biological mom Bianca and surely enough she has epilepsy stage 2 however, Chloe has stage 1. Her blood sugar was too high as well and I was forced to give her insulin for a few months because they thought she has diabetes. Later, we found out she didn't. But her oxygen was very low and she had to stay in that hospital now for 8 days. I was then forced with a decision and I had to leave my baby in the hospital overnight alone because I didn't have anyone to keep Daisy or Casey. I was dealing with a lot and I was losing my house because I got really behind, after all, that adoption cost me over ten thousand dollars.

So, at that point I was 28, and suffering from being a single mother to two sickly twins, I didn't have a father for them even though I was back together with Mook but they started calling him dad. He said he was fine with it and that made me closer to him which eventually led us to get married, but, I was having a hard time. The adoption caused division in my family and made my mom torn between two feuding children. She wanted me to work with her son Leroy with the girls but at this time I couldn't and I didn't want to. We did not see eye to eye and I wasn't going to allow him to run my house from outside. He was my brother, not my man and I was not his baby mama. See, when a man leaves behind his children and has a baby mama they can still flirt and make passes with one another because they might still have that soft side for each other but that was not my case. I never ever loved him in that manner so either he was going to be respectful or not and he chose not. I did once offer him a chance to act like an uncle to them until they were old enough to understand but he denied that suggestion. I understand his viewpoint but at this point, I didn't have room in my life for drama. I didn't want to interrupt their lives as they were really happy children. I don't think he will understand the difference between doing something for the children vs doing something for yourself. But I do what's in the best interest of the child. It is best that they continued to work on their development and learn and not worry about adult-like issues at age 5. So, I decided to proceed to raise them without him.

He had 3 other children and he wasn't financially supporting them. So,

I felt like he wouldn't make a difference in the twin's life. By this time, he filed the twins 5 years straight on his taxes even though they were under my care and that showed me enough about him to not want to even deal with him. He was fraudulent and money hungry. I didn't like people like that and I knew the struggle I had been through so I felt as though he should love them enough to allow us to get the money back from the daycare cost that was killing my pockets. I was paying $1,200 per month per child because they had special needs. One thing that people forget is that the state will help you while you are a foster mother, but the minute you adopt the children you receive zero assistance at all for them.

I was getting zero help from Leroy and my family would help babysit for me and until we starting dividing. I didn't feel safe around Leroy since he threatened my life so if he was around I didn't come around. I didn't care if it was Thanksgiving or Christmas. So, I began going to Mook's family house for all the holidays so that the twins could have a sense of family. We would open gifts with them and everything was fine until we end up separating. We were bound to separate though because Mook wanted to hang out every weekend like we used to but now I had 3 children to attend to and I couldn't. He also eventually told me he thought I should pay more bills than him because it's four of us and one of him. Now that I reflect on that, he was a real jerk. I am glad we are no longer together.

In short, the twins are now doing pretty well and healthy. They still struggle with asthma but, they are much better than they were. Living in Illinois during harsh winters really triggered their asthma. I still do not have a relationship with Leroy. I haven't told the twins that they are adopted just yet. But when they ask about being in my stomach I tell them that they were never in my stomach and they laugh and laugh. They think I am joking and when I see their face looking serious, I tell them they were in my butt to make them laugh. I do not know when the appropriate time is but I figure the more questions they ask me the more they will know. I plan to tell them their story in a book that I am putting together. I do watch movies with them about fostering and adoption so that they can understand the concept. They talk about it often with me and I know they are understanding more and more each day. But, my goal is to allow them to be children first. I raise my children to a different standard than most parents I know. See, my children are royalty in my eyes and I appreciate them. Therefore, having a mediocre or a half ass of a father for them isn't good enough. You must be all in or not in and cannot play with them. I love happy children, not miserable children. There is a big difference between the two and the last thing I want for them to feel is unwanted. They must feel wanted and loved. I do indeed believe they deserve that.

Love

One of my biggest issues is knowing what love feels like and what it is. My first time experiencing love was when I was 13 years old when I met Jay. I thought I was in love and even though it was puppy love, later in life it grew to real love. When I think of when a person understands love, it is usually about the time have a memory around age 5 and it is from their parents. Now, I always knew my parents loved me, especially my mom. But, I learned a lot about love over the years.

I began counseling when I was in almost ready to file a divorce and the counselor at that time made me take a quiz called the 5 love languages by Dr. Gary Chapman. I never even heard of this but I wanted to learn more about myself so I engaged. I took the test and found out that my love language is "Physical Touch". Which makes a world of sense when I was done. See physical touch does not mean intimacy, it means presence. My love language is constituted by the presence of others. Therefore growing up by myself always alone made me not know real love. When my father was not present for us, I didn't feel as loved as I should have been. Although my mom worked her behind off, she continued to call and check on me. She was present on most weekends and she made it to all my performances. That was important for me to feel loved. Her being at my performance showed her presence and my father not making it to not even one, showed me different. I felt like if it wasn't important for him to see me dance and compete in pom-pom competitions or even my cheer competitions growing up then he didn't love me. Now, this doesn't mean he didn't, and I know he did and he does love me. But, what matters is how I perceived love at a young age and I was clueless.

So, when I met Jay and his presence, I felt loved. Regardless if I was too young to know love or not, he was there. He would walk miles to meet me to get a hug or a kiss. He never pressured me to have sex with him or never pressured me to do anything. When Devon cheated, I didn't feel loved because he was living a double life. His double life meant he couldn't always be around. Devon also cheated on me with someone else outside of my friend and would bring Daisy around this new girl. He was way out of pocket for this. When Mook would leave me every Friday to go out with his friends and make excuses for why he couldn't spend the quality time I needed, I know then that he didn't love me. He would also spend Sundays with his mom and never invite me so he just wasn't present. He was also absent at our very own Marriage ceremony. I am not even sure why I didn't get our marriage annulled, but crazily I actually called the reverend who married us to ask what if I didn't turn in the paperwork and he said this has happened before but when the courts call he will tell them he did perform the ceremony. The reverend told me that it was best to file the paperwork and then annul it if that is what I wanted. I still wish to this day that I did because that relationship didn't have the foundation of love that it needed to make it last forever.

My issue at this point was that every man that I ever dealt with hurt me. My dad left my mom, Jay moved, Devon cheated with my close friend and a random chick, and Mook wasted 15 years of my life because he just wasn't ready to be a husband, family man, or leave the streets alone. So, I had no man to look up to because my stepfathers were all temporary and they just weren't invested enough to play a father role. They were all married to my mom and loved her but didn't truly bother with her three children as they should have. They were truly only in the marriage because my mom was so beautiful. Andrew lasted the longest as they were together for about 16 years but he suffered from substance abuse and was always gone. It wasn't until her last husband, Walter who was truly invested in having a real relationship with her children. But, by that time we were all grown and out of her house.

I learned so much from all the bad examples of what love was. I was also disappointed in my brother Leroy. That pain hurts on another level. He was supposed to protect me not take from me. Not threaten me or steal from me and the children. If you cannot trust your own brother, who could you trust? It is crazy to me because he walks around all the time mad at me and making statements like I stole his children from him. I always respond by stating, who in the heck wants to be a single mom at age 26 with three children? He left the girls in the system and so did Bianca. It took God to see me through as I was in over my head. It wasn't until I took control over my household and began to just treat the girls like my own and raise them to make things better.

The problem now is I had the girls for several years and now they are my children. Since I adopted them I get to choose who I want around them and what I want to do. I am not going to co-parent with my brother because he is not consistent. I wanted an example of how he would parent but I didn't get a good one from his other three children. They all have resentment towards him. Whomever I marry next will have to adopt them and be their father. Many people might disagree, but I must do what's best for the girls and me. I live a drama free life for the most part and I am in no mood to create new drama. It's not like Leroy is knocking over my door to see them. He barely calls and on average in the last 8 years, I received about 3 calls. That's being completely honest. I never missed one call from him and if I did, I always returned the calls. He provided fifty dollars two years ago through my mom and I purchased uniform pants. I know my mom protects him and makes him out to be this great guy but I believe in actions speak louder than words. If he is not doing enough for his other three children, then I can't see him doing enough for the twins. But I will tell them who he is when the time comes.

What Leroy did to me was show me that fathers can walk away from their children easily. What type of love is that I wonder? I don't want any parts of it plus as his sister, he showed me that he couldn't love me enough if he would treat me like he did. To this day, it still hurts. Big brothers are supposed to love their little sisters and protect them from harm not cause harm. Let me add that I also have an older brother who I admire who is older than Leroy and he was about the only example I had at this time. He is a hardworking man who takes care of his family and is dedicated to his marriage. But he was 5 years older than me and of course busy taking care of his responsibilities as he should. Now I do have other brothers and they are also dads. For the most part, my brothers don't play about their children. My baby brother in particular is an awesome dad and I admire him daily. We have the same dad but different moms. Unlike Leroy, whereas we have the same mom and dad.

Part of my point for illustrating the pain behind love for me is to show how different people love. When you are getting into a relationship, you don't look at these types of things but they are extremely important. Learning to love someone using their love language is important. If you do not use their love language, then they will not perceive the love you are trying to give them. I've been in a relationship where the person was buying me gift after gift and I didn't take it as love. I would consistently get reminded of what type of items they would purchase me because they love me. But, my love language was not that, it was presence. So, if you purchased me a diamond necklace and put it on my neck and minutes later, you were gone, then I didn't receive the love. Of course, I might have loved the necklace and even wore it, but if my love language is presence, you just showed me differently. You could have saved your money and planned a date to watch a movie and eat popcorn and I would have loved that better.

I am to a part in my life where I don't need to be bought. It is nice to receive gifts and all but the love I need is presence. I have finally got to a point where I can buy my own things and have enough to do so. Therefore, a man with time would be the best man for a person who love language is presence. If people learn their love language, there would be longer-lasting relationships and/or marriages. Learning how to love someone instead of hurt them is the best key. Due to the way each and every person grows up, love provided is completely different. So, when I reconnected with Jay, 21 years later I was stunned at the amount of attention and time he wanted to give me. Jay wanted to communicate with me and show me his love through invested time.

Now because Jay is a provider, of course, he wants to take care of me and even buy me things. But, how he shows love is paying attention to little things and giving me all his time. Some things that he does is extremely precious. For an example, if we are sitting and talking, he is looking into my eyes, holding my hands, and he even moves my hair out of my face. Now, of course, I wear sew-ins as protective styles, and he treats my sew-in like it was grown out of my head. He rubs on my hair like it is mine. Most black women who wear extensions have issues with men touching their hair because they are too busy trying to find out if it is weave and that is annoying. But, not Jay, he just doesn't care. Whenever I am taking my hair down he wants to sit and talk to me and watch the entire process. It used to be annoying to me but, now it makes the process goes by faster cause we are talking about everything. Once my hair is done again, he immediately becomes my hype man. It's funny to me because I used to be his cheerleader growing up and for this small time, we switch places. He knows how much I love doing my own hair. So, it is cute that he does this. He always tells me that I am first. He makes a point to show me this because he taught me if you're not first you are last. I have to thank him for showing me so much love and attention because of his patience with me being damaged goods from a failed relationship and hurtful family issues, I know pure love. It will take me some time to get myself together to be the best woman I can for him as well. With everything I have been through, I have to take time out to heal.

Healing

I had to heal the pain, scars, and disappointment that I have encountered. I had to heal the foolishness and deal with my unfortunate childhood. I had to heal from the storm that I faced alone to learn myself all over again. I went through so many changes and moved so much throughout my childhood that I lost a lot along the way. One of the biggest things I ever had to deal with besides divorce, is being an adoptive mother. Everything has been all over the place my entire life. I have managed to make it look good, but it has not been easy. I have never been a negative person nor do I throw people under the bus. I keep everything locked into myself due to my trust issues. My trust issues started from not having that consistent male in my life that I can trust in my childhood to my multiple disappointments with the men in my life. The way I heal is through writing. I have never been one to throw my business on social media and I only post positive things. People don't want to always see drama on your timeline or even hear about it on the phone.

Therefore, I typically just write in my journal to get me through rough times. It is hard to open up to people even friends. I have been burned by almost every person I call a friend except one or two people. I have got into an argument with all of my friends one way or another, all I believe except Cara, my friend of 18 years. I think my expectations are too high for friendships or I always put more in than I get out of them. It is also hard to deal with females regularly because they are catty, messy, or not realistic.

Growing up and moving around I met many new friends. I preferred to keep my same friends I met in like 3rd-5th grade. They were the friends I felt I could relate to and the most loyal. I only kept under a handful of friends even though I know many people believe that I am the popular type and very social. I believe my bubbly attitude makes me likable and my positive vibes make me tolerable. While healing I had to realize that not everyone is my friend today. Now, I will not take from my friendships throughout the years, but, I have developed into a new person and I am not the same person I once was. I have changed dramatically and I believe divorce did this to me. I began to realize when I went through my divorce how I was alone and not many people checked on me. That in itself allowed me to weed out who really is there for me and who is not. It is crazy because I have always had myself together financially so I never needed to borrow anything and for the most part, because I am so private, I wouldn't need emotional support. But, when I finally needed someone's ear to be there and listen, I literally heard crickets. Everyone was so busy all of a sudden and I have to thank everyone for being busy. What it did for me was make me extremely strong.

I know that the friends that I have kept along the way were amazing when we were younger but the person I am today is not the same me I was then. Therefore, some of my friendships I had to distant myself, and some I had to walk away to fully heal. See, some of my friendships were very toxic. It would get to the point, whereas I couldn't even put my finger on why my friendships were breaking off but I do know that when God wants you to grow, he makes you uncomfortable. I have never been so uncomfortable in my life. But, I did realize that I was the friend to everyone that I needed them to be and they just couldn't measure up. I know that I will always love the women who I spent the majority of my life around, but sometimes you outgrow people.

I remember my friend Nya was talking to me about aggressive friendships. I had to really think about this because when she approached me I felt offended like she was referring to me. But, she just didn't know what to say but she wanted to protect my feelings. But, really what she did was let me know a few things that stuck with me. One, she felt that I was too aggressive at this time and typically I am not. Two, she taught me that one of my other friends was actually way too aggressive and has been my whole life. Now, Nya was right, I was too aggressive in my friendship at the time of my divorce because I needed someone to be there for me. I needed someone to help me heal. Instead of looking to her, I should have looked to God. There is no man alive that can help you heal from pain or a broken heart but God and time. There is no bandaid or quick fix that will help you heal. But, when you finally heal you will feel way better than when you first started.

Another friendship I had to heal from was the friendship I shared with my friend Tangie. Tangie and I were as close as anyone can get, but when we got older and we looked at life, religion, and everything else differently. The love I have for Tangie is irreplaceable. There will never be another person like her because although we stayed into it, we bonded on another level. She was family, period. Our families were close, and she was like a sister to me. But, we grew apart and I am perfectly fine with it. I believe that she just didn't understand me after my divorce and I didn't understand the new level of spirituality that she was undergoing.

But for almost 30 years, she was my best friend and my sister from another mister. It was hard to walk away from her because of the love I have for her but, our relationship is not the same and I know now that we will forever get into it. I would never blast her on social media even though she tried me. But, our toxic friendship started around the time I was getting married and just never got better. It hurt to completely stop talking to someone you talk to all day and all night. We were like serious home girls like the show Girlfriends or Waiting to

Exhale. I really wanted to walk away without conflict because I never want to hurt anyone, and you never know when you need someone. I am the one to always try to avoid altercations. It took me a very long time to realize that we are way too different. In my last book, Independently Foolish, I quoted that, "Opposites do not attract, they divide", this goes for friendships too.

I had to heal from this relationship because I wasn't learning anything or gaining anything. For the first time, I was tired of always being the strongest in my group. I want to learn as well. For the most part, though, my friends were established and had careers such as a nurse, flight attendant, and an education administrator. They are homeowners as well and I was very proud of them all. But I realized that if I friend likeminded people, I can't get far as I would like in life. Nothing further than where we were. But, if I friend people who are of a different caliber or level in life, I can grow and learn. That saying that states if you hang around 5 millionaires, you can be the 6th is basically where I am now. It is nothing personal, but where I am mentally is reaching for the stars. I am naturally a female hustler and I am always thinking of what I need to do next. I will never stop reaching or getting to the next level in life.

Therefore, I had to walk away from my everyday attachments of my friends to checking in with them here and there, while I surround myself in an unfamiliar environment. I love to hangout and I always will have love for my homegirls, but I can thank Nya for setting the bar high for me. She showed me so much in one small text message that I am forever grateful. It made me take a step back to figure out my life and get it together. It was really hard to do this, but, I have to now surround myself with women who are bosses and entrepreneurs and then I will be able to learn. I have a different insight on life and I have matured so much. Like my bishop Larry Darnell Trotter would say, "What's to come is better than what's been". I am looking forward to what's to come for me and I know that it will be big. Mentally, I am just on a whole new level and I am approaching this level with open arms.

So, what I needed to heal from was my childhood, my relationships, my former marriage, close family, and my friends. I would say I went through a full cleaning. I needed to do this healing to move forward. I do believe in the fact that you cannot keep doing the same things and expect different results. You must change something if you are not happy. Part of my healing was truly just spending time alone and learning who I was and what I like and didn't like. I needed to get from up under everyone to think. How often does anyone ever get a chance to do this? I had a hard time even figuring out what I liked.

I have been through counseling and even trying to meditate. But, the only thing that worked when it came to me was praying. Recently my father apologized to me for missing valuable time growing up and I can honestly say that was a big weight lifted off my shoulders. Part of the reason why it helped me was that he did it in front of my younger sister. Part of my issue with my father was watching him be an incredible father to my younger sisters Mandy and Ariel. This was tough for me and I don't think no one knew it. My father would send me pictures in the mail of just him, Mandy, and Ariel. Now, I was happy for my sisters to have a better experience than I did. It was good for them to get more time with our dad, but for me, it wasn't always easy.

My father is a militant man who had a prominent career with the US Marshals Service and I am very proud of him. I want him to know that I am just like him in many ways. My dad has earned his bachelor's degree and his master's degree. He lives in a rather large home that has a movie theater and an office, etc. He doesn't have a tolerance for non-sense, and he will cut you off if you make yourself untrustworthy. He is blunt, and rather honest and is a good example of a man. He just valued his career early on in his life and now values family. It took me several years to understand this and although I am happy he values family now, I wish he valued family when I was younger. Nevertheless, his apology was very sincere, and I forgave him. It made me tear up and I did smile to know he cared enough to apologize. I needed that apology to grow. This big weight I have been carrying on my shoulders truly held me back. I didn't want to carry it on my shoulders any longer, so I had to let go and accept my life like it was and allow my heart to heal. A big part of healing is forgiveness. Most times, I can forgive, I just don't forget much.

I am still working on myself in regards to my brother Leroy. I forgave him a very, very long time ago. I just don't trust him much so it might appear that I haven't forgiven him, but I have and God knows this. My biggest concern with him is consistency and the mere fact that I don't play around with children. See, you can make or break a child by providing an unsafe or unhealthy childhood. The twins do not know who he is nor do they know their biological mother. Since I have legally adopted them, I get to make a choice rather I want to be bothered with all that and I feel like it is not the time. Many might disagree, including my own mother Bonnie Ann, but, it is not her decision to make. I love my mom and I love all my family and friends, but anyone's opinion on how I run my household or raise my children doesn't matter anymore.

Everyone had a chance to raise their children the best way they see fit. My choice is to raise them in a loving, safe, drama-free household. Free from confusion and pain and when they get to an age where they can handle the entire truth, then I will reveal their entire life story to them. Part of my healing was to step up and fight for the rights I earned. I do not receive an ounce of child support for the twins nor have I ever therefore, there is no way in the world, I couldn't live the way someone else wants me to and be completely happy. I had to heal my heart from all the wounds of this adoption and move forward in life living my way. It took time to get here as well and it wasn't easy. I had to learn to step away and distance myself from anyone who is causing me stress. Adopting the twins caused division in my entire family. I felt as though everyone wanted Leroy in the twin's life but he had no efforts to do so and filing children on your taxes that you are not caring for, isn't love. That is simply greed in which I want no parts of period. I cannot be around people who commit fraud or acts of fraud. It is insulting and it questions my integrity, and I will not have that. I cannot cheat the government or the internal revenue service to collect some money that can result in jail. I am not made like that so I healed from the pain from my decision of being an adoptive mother and accepting it.

I had to learn to be okay with my decisions and live with them. Part of my healing was learning to be okay with other people's negative deception of me. This was by far the hardest pain. I have always had this clean woman image and I always want to do what's right and make everyone happy. This is not possible. Not in all cases and therefore, I was going to leave someone unhappy for me to be happy. See, I know that I would typically live unhappily just to make everyone around me happy. I have always been this overachiever and I wanted to always be there for everyone. For the majority of my life, I had plenty of time for everyone. I didn't know until my friend Tangie told me that I am always there for everyone because I had an absent husband. She was absolutely right and often the truth hurts, but this didn't hurt me, but it did set me straight. Now, I know it is okay to not always be there for everyone. Especially when they are not there for you. Going through a divorce was by far the most hurt I experienced in my entire life. It was a shocking moment for a lot of people who had no clue that I was going through it behind closed doors. It was shocking to my dad, my grandmother, and even my friends. Since I had to learn to heal from a broken heart all alone, I just decided it was best to be alone in my everyday life. For the most part, I stay all to myself. There are cons and pros to this and I learned to live with it. The best part is no drama, no judgment, and no explaining yourself. The con is it dampens your social life and it also can be lonely at times. The lonely part is not too bad once you get used to it. I do believe it was all a part of my healing process to make me into a stronger being.

The very last stage of my healing process was new love. I was not looking for it, I was trying to reject it. But, it came in the most pure form of love. When I got reunited with Jay after 21 years of being away from each other, we began to talk on the phone for hours. He explained to me all of the triumphs he experienced and to my surprise, they were quite similar. Since he didn't live in the same state as me all we had was our conversations. It was just what I needed especially as a recent divorcee. I was in no shape to be with someone every day when I was healing. Our conversations were deep and we connected mentally. He shared with me some of the most embarrassing stories and he was brutally honest. He was so honest, that he jeopardized losing me just to tell the truth. He gained my respect from that day forward and we have been the best of friends ever since.

What I know is that he too had been healing and stripped of everything just like myself. He also had not many friends, well, basically none. So, here we were with very limited communication with the outside world but each other. What we did over the next 16 months was to heal each other. He shared with me the areas he thought I needed to heal and I shared with him the areas he needed to heal. We worked day in and day out with each other by discussing ways we could have done everything better. We analyze every single thing about our past and even our past relationships. We didn't shy away from saying what was right and what was wrong. Jay has a very strong bonded family and they were very monumental in my healing. Since my divorce, I have lost an entire family for myself and the children. So, when God brought me and Jay back together he knew exactly what I needed. Jay's entire family accepted me with open arms. His cousins, siblings, and parents were very kind and invited me to everything. They began to call me family and it was exactly what I needed.

They gave me the gift of love and it helped me heal. Jay grew up in the church just like me, except he is the pastor's son. Therefore he was at church three times as much as I was. But, the first thing he did for me upon reuniting was praying for me. He prayed really hard and we connected spiritually. There is something about a God-fearing man that is a turn on for me. Jay didn't just tell me he believes in God, he showed me. Jay reads a lot and he reads to me daily affirmations to keep me motivated. He compliments me every day and reminds me that I am loved. He never tells me no and I don't think he even knows that word. He is extremely sweet and handsome. He is truly my baby and I am forever grateful for him taking his time with me and allowing me to heal without stressing me out further.

His level of support is amazing for me and I began to get mad at myself for blocking my own blessing by staying in a relationship that has been over. I could not get to the blessing God had for me until I let go and trusted God. I have God to thank for this union and even during the craziest of times during the pandemic, Jay and I remain close. I can honestly say that he is indeed my very best friend and he is all mine. I don't have to fight for him or argue. I don't have to guess anything because he is so upfront and honest he gave me everything I needed. What he gave me is full access to him. All passwords, bank accounts, and time. I have no worries and it feels extremely weird because I had no clue that this was possible. But, it is and I am finally happy. I can honestly say that when Beyoncé said, when the worlds at a war, let our love heal us all, I completely understand. My world was turned upside down unexpectedly and I fought with everyone, for every reason. But, when I found real love, it was the only thing that could help me connect with a male like I have been longing for my entire life. I can thank Jay a million times over and it still won't be enough. But I can say, as soon as we are married, I am going to give that man some babies. This man was my soul mate all along. He is perfect for me in every way and because of his love, and God's love, I am healed. I love him.

Independent Lessons

learned so much over the last decade and I can honestly say, writing is a great tool and it can help others. You never know what someone is going through in their life, and everything that looks like glitter, isn't gold. From my childhood events, I learned a lot about myself and why I had so many issues with men. See, the lack of fatherhood in the family household, allowed my judgment and selection of men to be misguided. I didn't have a good start to finding out exactly what standards I should have. The lesson behind all this is to ensure that we break generational curses and show our children how a strong family looks. Since I have already made a mistake by marrying the wrong man, I have already carried the same tradition as my mother. I stayed in my last relationship for fifteen years and when I met Mook, Daisy was 2 years old therefore, she was also provided a poor example. Luckily her father Devon is around but, he too didn't provide a good example in the beginning. It took us time to get our co-parenting together. It is not very easy to work together but if you do it for the best interest of the child it will work out. See, there are many lessons in life that you can get from learning about someone else's story. You can learn that you are not the only one going through things.

There are always two sides to every story and everyone has different perspectives on life and handling situations. But, providing some guidance from my perspective might help someone dealing with issues in their life that can eventually lead to depression. Or worst, finding yourself not really being genuinely happy with yourself and your life. Sometimes you have to take a step back and really think about all the events in your life. Evaluate what events in your life have helped shaped you into the person you are today. There is nothing wrong with change. If you are the same as you have always been, then you are not elevating. I was once told by an ex that I am always changing and that they never change. Well, that is not a good thing. That means that you are stagnant without growth. Well, that is why we didn't work out. I am going to provide you with 7 easy lessons to help you grow in life to take along your way.

Lesson #1 Confront Your Childhood/Past

What issues in your past do you have that you are holding onto? It could be daddy issues like I had, and if so, confront it! It could be anything under the sun, but take time to analyze what it is and figure out what will make you heal and feel better. My childhood struggle prevented me from knowing how to choose the right man and I always chose the wrong one. I moved around a lot, lost friends due to the moving, and had multiple stepparents. I probably have more step brothers and sisters than anyone in the world. I had to find out what will make me heal from my childhood and it took me many years to figure this out. It wasn't until my dad actually apologized for his absence until I realized it would be the only way to let go of the pain I was holding onto.

I cannot change the past, but I can learn to cope with it knowing that my dad was apologetic. His absence created a domino effect for me. So many things in my life just were not in place due to his absence. This showed me how important it is to have a father in the household. So, if you can keep your family together, please do. So many African American families separate so easily without a fight or even counseling. For some reasons, black men feel like they don't need counseling or can't nobody tell them anything. But, this is not true and I found that counseling truly helps your mental health and, most importantly, it shows you how to communicate effectively. Many times we think that counseling is ineffective and cannot do anything to help a relationship, but it can. Counseling teaches you effective ways to communicate so that you can work on your relationships and communicate your feelings successfully.

I realized in counseling that I had many issues within myself that needed fixing and because I too was in a relationship with poor communication, I couldn't relay how I felt. In fact, I felt insecure most of my life even when in most times there was nothing wrong with me. All that mattered was that I wasn't happy with myself and honestly that stemmed from my childhood. I remember talking to my sister Ariel about my issues regarding our father, and she told me she thought it would be a great idea to talk it out. But, this was before he apologized to me for his absence. I considered talking it out, but I knew that wouldn't heal me. I knew I would be healed when I was set free from the person who caused the pain in my childhood. I know that when my father took responsibility for his actions, I would be fine. When he did so my heart smiled, and although I had tears, it was more tears of joy. I always wondered would he ever acknowledged his wrong, and he did. Now our relationship is amazing but it didn't get this way overnight.

I didn't write this book to bash my father either. He is an excellent provider and a great man. But, sometimes you can suffer silently and do more damage to yourself. I couldn't figure out what was wrong with me until I started writing and then I figured it out. Confronting your past is a very hurtful process and if it deals with other family members, it can cause some hesitancy on older relatives. I know this firsthand and I still have unanswered questions about my biological grandfathers on both my maternal and paternal sides in which I have never met nor do I know who they are. Sadly, my parents don't know either. So, when I think of my childhood,

I can also think of theirs and feel that they went through matters way worse than me. This could be the issue my father had growing up and so the cycle continued through me. It is just one touchy topic that has to resolve one way or the other. Hopefully, in most cases, issues are resolved. But, considering life is way too short, I don't personally think it is a good idea to hold on to past hurt. I definitely had to let go of some past hurt to flourish and grow and I must say ever since I did so, I have been glowing.

Lesson # 2 Find Yourself

The lesson to learn is before you find someone, find yourself! Make sure you know who you are and if you don't know, you are not in a position to be in a relationship. How can you be a good wife or husband to anyone if you don't know yourself? You must know your likes and dislikes and even your goals in life. But, you also have to know what to look for when it comes to finding someone to love. The best advice is to be sure to look into someone's childhood and how they were raised to aid you. You must know how your significant other was raised! Mook's parents lived separated for 30 years. This was one of our biggest issues. We lived separately for 10 years, and we even lived separated while married. Sounds foolish I know but, I couldn't be mad at him for wanting to live like this when this was the example he was provided. Mook felt that as long as we had keys to each other places, then we can live separately just fine. I still don't know how I let that slide.

In contrast, in my childhood, I moved around a lot and I also experienced a few stepfathers. This is instrumental in discovering who I was. For any man that wanted to marry me, it was important to know that I might want to move around a lot. I also am not in fear of divorce. I do not want to get another divorce, but I watched both my parents get divorced multiple times. If Mook would have considered my childhood, then he should have known that I had no problem with leaving him after he acted a complete fool and/or getting a divorce. That is exactly why I filed for divorce. See men think that women will continue to deal with their mistreatment. Not every woman is weak or scared to be alone. Although I am very happy with my decision, I prefer not to get divorced. I had to find myself before I was any good for anyone. After being in a failed relationship for 15 years, this task wasn't easy. I went through many changes to find the true beauty inside my own self. I had to repair the teardown from my prior relationship. I am sure anyone can relate to the "tear down". This is when the person you are with or no longer with, tell you what you will not find in someone else. Or what's worst when they tell you that no one else will deal with you or treat you like they once did. Well, I have heard it all before and it took time to find myself after finding out that everything I was told was a complete lie. I was told that no one would want to be with me and three children. Well, the devil is a liar because there are plenty of men that would be with a woman with 3 children. So, we as a people have to stop listening to people tell us about what we are capable of and we also have to stop believing them. When I stopped believing in the lies, is when I began to find myself and learn to love myself for who I was and not what I was to someone else.

Lesson #3 Seek Answers in Relationships with How They Were Raised

When I began to continue my relationship with Jay, the first thing I did was consider his childhood and his parent's relationship. When Jay told me that they were still together, then I knew that he would also want to replicate a long-lasting marriage. I also needed someone to level me out. I wanted to be able to learn and this is exactly what happened.

The next thing I needed to look at is how a man treats his children. In my previous relationship with Mook, he was a good dad when it came to helping for paying for things for his children. He would pay for somethings for them but he didn't go out of his way to sacrifice everything. He didn't invest enough time with them in their childhood either. I knew that Mook loved his children, but he not being completely present was a red flag that I ignored. I was happy with knowing he didn't run away from his responsibilities, but that wasn't good enough. It is good we didn't have children together because I couldn't expect anything more than what he offered his other children. When I got with Jay, I learned so much about what type of father he was. I loved to hear that he took his children to school daily and provided for them financially 100%. He even purchased a home cash for them to live in with their mom in Indiana. I earned so much respect for him and I am so glad that he took care of his children. This showed me that he wanted to be sure that they were taken care of regardless and now there is no mortgage for the children's mother to pay. To me, this is better than child support and I would take this over child support any day. Jay is the perfect example of a really good man. So, if any ladies are reading this book, please do not settle. It is good men out there and it is very important to look into their childhood and their history to get a full picture of what your life will look like. Believe me, when I say, a tiger doesn't change his stripes.

If you are struggling with finding a good man one of the reasons is because you didn't do your research on his childhood. Another reason is you didn't consider yours. There is no way a person whose parents didn't live together during their marriage and a person whose parents get divorced and remarried quite frequently would work. There are apparent commitment issues between both of us. You have to learn to use a technique I call "the fast forward" move. In a fast forward technique, you fast forward to guess ending possibilities. It is like the, "what would happen if I got with this guy type of thing"? You should look at two different possible scenarios. Like we could work out or separate. But if we work out, what does that look like in five years or even ten? If we separate what would I be missing? Women fail by using our imagination to look at fairytales way too often. We jump head into these relationships that we know are a dead-end situation. We make these men something they never were. We are lying to ourselves and our friends and families. We need to be more honest with ourselves and stop this foolishness. It cost nothing, to be honest with yourself. I had to learn this the hard way and I kept covering up for a man who wasn't worthy.

Lesson # 4 Run from the "Dutch" Type

Another lesson I need to share is the lesson of this thing called "DUTCH". Who made this up and why is my question? I cannot stand for a man to go dutch with me on everything. For those who don't know, dutch is when you are both paying half on everything. Now, I know some people are struggling and I get it, it works well. But, how do you as a woman be submissive to a man when you both have equal responsibilities? I think that the question of the day is how long are you supposed to participate in dutch responsibilities? What I have learned in my life is that it is hard to deal with a dutch relationship.

Now don't get things twisted, dutch does work when you are young and you both are trying to find yourself. I did it and I was fine with it, but eventually you should transition away from this type of situation. I invested 15 years and wasted plenty of time in this type of situation.

Now in the beginning Mook wasn't the dutch type, but eventually he turned into one and couldn't shake it. It got so bad that eventually he changed to paying absolutely nothing. So, that is when I had to leave that situation alone because there is no way a man could ever live off me. I could no longer sleep next to a man who thought it was remotely close to not pay absolutely anything. Even asking me to pay the full mortgage for a few months was out of line if you ask me. I am not supposed to pay the full mortgage with a husband and still expect me to act like a wife. There were clearly some gender role responsibility differences here.

What bothers me most about men not taking their roles seriously, is the fact that they want to make decisions in a household they are not paying for. You cannot make executive decisions without being an executor! This is why they have employers and managers. Employers follow leadership under management. Same theory in the household. You want someone to follow you, then you must be a leader. Most men want to have the royal king treatment inside the household. If you are indeed the king in the household, it's because you have decided to boss up and actually be a king. Being a boss requires you to consume the full mortgage or pay for the home that we live in.

I don't like it when men think that dutch is the way and have no intent on being a provider. This is selfish in my eyes and it is quite unfair. In a man's eyes a woman is supposed to cook, clean, wash clothes, and tend to the children. But, you mean to tell me that women also have to work and pay half the bills too? I believe the role of the woman is unfair. I don't think that a woman will fully respect a man who doesn't take his role or responsibilities seriously enough. Once this happens, women typically are very opinionated and we are arguing more and more every day. News flash to the men that are reading this, women don't need a roommate and we can definitely do badly all by ourselves. We don't need a man to make us do worse than we are already doing by ourselves. At this point then the relationship is pointless.

Lesson #5 Know Your Worth

This right here is quite important because we struggle with this daily. Once you have found yourself and you know your likes and dislikes, it is very important to know what you are worth. Find out what value you bring to your relationship. If you don't know what your worth is, then you have a lot of work and you still need to find yourself. But, if it helps you to create a list and write down everything you bring to the relationship, then do so.

I must share a story about a woman I knew who also always seem to find the wrong type of man. Now, I was just like her at one point in my life but, if you think about all the factors in your childhood, their childhood, and you want to get married, but still can't. Let me tell you why. First and foremost, no matter what man I come across in my life, he will forever talk about marriage to me and you know why? It is because just like when you applying for a job, you have to complete an application and you inform the company you are applying to what qualifications you possess. I will always be like I have 3 degrees, and I have 12 years' experience, I know how to do this efficiently, etc. Well, the same thing apply to relationships.

Don't be surprised by this and take heed to what I am about to say so that it can help you further in life. This is what I call free game. But, the woman that I know has made many mistakes. See, women want a man to marry them, but their relationship resume sucks! Some women bounce around to many different men, let every single last one of them meet their children instantly, and worst, they are unstable. If you cannot provide for your own self, and you are fully dependent you will attract the same type of no good men. You cannot look for a good quality man, because you are not of good quality. You cannot keep a man that you slept with the first night. You have set your bar too low and gave him everything in one week. Well, now he is done with you and now you have to start over. See, he probably liked you in the beginning and he also thought you were probably cute, and I believe you probably are, but you failed at knowing your worth and now he doesn't know it either.

Yes, I have gotten divorced recently but it wasn't because I didn't know my worth. It was because I knew exactly what I was worth and I can't allow a worthless man to change that for me. I am not giving out lessons that I haven't learned myself. I typically walk away without giving a second chance because there is no way in the world I will keep getting done wrong. I stand up for what I believe in and I have learned not to settle. So, when I watch this young woman that I knew struggle to find the right man, I wonder does she know her worth. In a relationship you have time. You don't have to always have sex with everyone. You can try to be cool, do all types of things for that man, and he still won't marry you.

Some other reasons are because you are not established enough. If you are too dependent, men feel that you are too much work and they don't want to deal with it. They don't mind dealing with some issues but it would be nice for you to have a consistent job, a roof over you or your children's head if you have children, and provide for your own self. Men dream just like women dream and if you are not capable of helping them build their empire, they don't want you. They are looking at what you can add to them, not what you can take from them. Women have these men need to pay for my nails, hair, and feet mentality. It is so minor and it is sad. You should already have your damn hair, feet, and nails done. How about you present yourself as you got it together so he can learn about you instead, of pay for you. With payment comes certain responsibilities and expectations that prevent you from actually finding quality men. So, for my ladies, please ask yourself what it is he wants you for? What do you have that he doesn't? What can you add to his life to make things better? But, be sure to have it together for a man that is not a dutch man otherwise you are wasting time with him.

Part of knowing your worth in my eyes is keeping your legs closed to see if the person you are trying to get with can wait for you or are you just another number? You can learn a lot about being in a relationship when you are abstinent. I bet this is too farfetched, right? It really is not and the reason most relationships don't work is we as human beings are too weak for flesh. How can you trust this man to go anywhere without you, if he cannot hold it together for you. The men that are too thirsty to get in your pants are very thirsty for the next female. It is all fun and games until you don't trust him and then find yourself acting crazy cause you don't know if he cheating. So, please before you drive yourself crazy try keeping your legs closed and actually get to know the person you are dating. Stop mimicking all the reality television and realize that your life is as real as it gets. Don't just throw it to anyone. Save yourself for someone worth it. I didn't think I could do it myself, but now since I am waiting for marriage, and saving myself, I am seeing much better results mentally.

Any man that is willing to wait for you is already learning your worth and he already values you. He might be around for the chase and the thrill, but if you hold off, he could leave or he could stay. If he chooses to stay, he is definitely worth keeping. We are telling and teaching our daughters to wait for marriage, but cannot do it ourselves. That is very contradictory and should be changed. We as a people don't even date anymore! We got straight to the bed and that is not the answer to finding the right man or knowing your worth. In the end, all you feel is alone and that is an empty feeling. Once that man gets what he wants from you more than likely his actions will change and guess what you get next? A bunch of excuses.

Lastly, women, we got to stop giving these men a million years to marry us. I waited to discuss this topic because if a man doesn't value marriage, you are wasting your damn time. But, we know our worth and still, we decided to be this fake wife and give a man everything, thinking it would pay off in a ring. It will not! I waited 10 years to get married, and then stayed legally married 5 years, and then it was a wrap. That shows me that I shouldn't have wasted 10 years being a glorified girlfriend giving a man "the husband treatment" that he didn't deserve. I didn't do anything but waste my damn time and lost out on all of my 20's and half of my 30's. It doesn't take that long to decide to be married. If you look into their childhood and don't see their family married in long-lasting mentally healthy relationships, then you might want to call it quits.

You also need to just ask the man does he want to get married or ask him when. Stop playing with yourself mentally because this will result in you devaluing yourself and not knowing your own worth. If his response to getting married in one day, then that is about how long it should take you to pack your things and move right along. I want to know if you are worth my time or not. If he doesn't like to discuss marriage then move around because you will not get married to him ever. If he is not ready or mature enough to see that type of life with you and that is perfectly fine. Appreciate his honesty and move on with your life. It will be wasted if he doesn't want to talk about it. If he gets mad when you discuss marriage or the future, he is the one you want to leave immediately. Marriage is something I am not shying away from in any conversation. Actually, my guy currently talks about marriage more than me and he lights up like a

Christmas tree upon discussing it. He loves to plan the wedding and talk about what he wants to happen. Trust me it is better when the goal is mutual. Just do me, one favor ladies, know your worth, keep it, and enjoy it.

Lesson #6 Never Settle

This is by far the most important of the lessons. Many of us know what we want and how we want things. For most women, we have a whole list of things we want from the man we want to spend the rest of our lives with. Men, know the qualities they want their potential wife to be to possess. Often no one finds what they want in totality. Many of us find someone and pick some of the things we require from a partner in a relationship. I know for myself I was stuck on the fact that my ex wasn't bothering my girls nor was he beating on me, so I settled. This is what we all do because we have a fear of being alone. We date just to have some comfort and some company.

Many people have hidden agendas in these relationships. Not only is comfort a factor, but so is convenience. The convenience of splitting the bills or even convenient living arrangements. Most women have themselves together and have their own places. Many men, not all, still live with family, parents, or even a roommate. So, yes it is easy to move together when you didn't work hard to obtain your own place. It is also easy to go from living with a family member to a woman who will pretend to be your wife and serve you as if you are the king of her castle. This was definitely my situation. I settled because my ex was willing to live with me in the home that I purchased. I was comfortable with my name being the only name on the house. He never had to finance a house so he didn't appreciate all the hard work I did to obtain it. So he was easily able to move in with me and get treated like a king in a castle he didn't have to do a damn thing to earn.

See, he always wanted to purchase

cash homes to live in, and there is nothing wrong with that. But buying cash homes with limited funds leaves you in bad neighborhoods. This was the case for him. I would rather finance a house in a very nice neighborhood and pay a mortgage, to live comfortably. It is a great concept, to have zero mortgage payments, but when the neighborhoods are Englewood or Roseland in Chicago, I prefer to stay in an area my children can attend better schools and obtain a great education. I am a firm believer of you get what you pay for.

The reality of my former situation is that we were a full mismatch and I settled to be with him, just to have someone. I had many qualities that any man would love, but to be with me, you have to be a certain type of man. I can no longer settle for just any type of man. Not after earning my Ph.D. and already being established. What we women often do is fall in love with our own imagination of what we think our man has the potential to be and that is how we settle. I think many men have the potential to be anything they want, but the key is that they have to want to do so. If they are telling you they have dreams that is one thing. But, they have to also have the hustle and the pursuit to go along with that. This goes the same for men who have a woman that cries about what she wants to do, but never pursue those dreams and blames her being a mom for the reason. When you are with someone who is a dreamer but, not a pursuer, you have done nothing but used your imagination to make this person better in your own mind. The reality is that the person you are with might just have great ideas with no motivation and in most cases not desire to actually do anything. So what you have is a space filler that is not fulfilling to your space.

Consequently, you spend years in a relationship unhappy because you have settled. You have settled with someone that has some, but not all of the things you want in a spouse. You have convinced yourself that there will never be anyone perfect for you, but that is nothing further from the truth. There is someone perfect for you but you are still with the person who isn't and currently blocking your blessings. You can lie to everyone in your circle, but you cannot lie to yourself. You cannot find the right one, while you are stuck on the wrong one. To move forward, you need to learn to stop settling. You cannot get to the level you want to reach, because you have shortened and cheated yourself.

Last, this is for the women who are with a man since they have children together. I am very happy that you have taken the time to stay with your child's father and taken a sacrifice for your family. But, you cannot be the only one always sacrificing. A woman will settle with being unhappy just to say they are still with their child's father or to show other women on social media that they are a so-called family. I understand the need to have the father in the household but do know that once the children grow up and get out of the house, you will more than likely be miserable. I have seen it time and time again. It is a huge step to take to walk away with children together and I am a product of a single mother, but the one thing I do remember and it helped me throughout my life is watching my mother get divorced. Many people see this as a bad thing, however, the fact of the matter is that my mom refuses to settle. If you are not a good match, she will not stick around and she will leave your behind as fast as she got into the relationship. This is something she has instilled in me and although I am like her in many ways, I still have a tendency to settle in many ways. The point is to find someone worthy so you are not settling. It is also important before you have children to find a quality parent to raise children with so that they don't grow up having a void like I did as a child. The only way to change generational curses is to make wiser choices and take the time to plan out all possibilities.

Last, I think my biggest issue is trying

to make sure that I am not so rough on men and my expectations are not too high whereas I am always settling. I was looking for someone close to baby Jesus perfection. I had to realize that I am not asking for too much. When I created a list of things I wanted in a man, a husband, my list was very typical. I wanted a man that is a provider, who doesn't want me to do dutch with him on everything, someone who wanted to spend quality time with me without pressure, someone who genuinely loved my children as their own, and last someone who is God-fearing, and it shows. I think my list was extremely fair, but I settled on some of the things I wanted. When I created the list I forgot to mention one thing and that was baby mamas. This is very important as well because a baby mama can run you away with all the drama they bring to your life and relationship. So, I also wanted to be with someone who had a good, healthy relationship with their child's mother and have established boundaries, with effective co-parenting already in place.

This was the area I always settled in and I don't know why. I always say eventually time will heal all wounds or if the baby mama gets a man they will move on. Trust me when I say this is not true. If the person you are with have children and their baby mama is unruly and dramatic, she will be that same way the entire relationship. Baby mamas are sneaky and they often settle for being second or a side chick just to have a piece of what they used to have in your man. I have experienced baby mamas and the bitter ones are all the same. They send pictures of themselves to your man as if the man doesn't know what she looks like, sneaky messages, and always slick passes. They want to know and confirm if he is still thinking about them, love them, or miss them. It is sad, but I have yet to be proven wrong. So, when you decide to date a man with children, be prepared to date his baby mama. She is now y'all baby mama. There is no separation in this, so get used to it, or leave, because if not, you will be in for a lifetime, and guess what, you just settled yet once again! Remember and take heed about settling. There is no way to be truly happy when you have decided to accept less than what you deserve. It makes perfect sense to get what you want out of life so that you are fulfilled and happy. After all, life is what you make it.

Lesson #7 Learn How to Love

The last lesson is to learn how to love. One of my biggest issues is that I grew up independently and most time alone and unaccompanied. I had to learn how to love alone because the love I was displayed while I was raised was not the love that I wanted to provide to my children, my future husband, or my family. You only get one chance to raise your children and the time goes by so fast. Learning their love language and how they love will help you grow and make an everlasting effect on your child forever.

You are responsible for your children and there is no way telling them and showing them you love them will hurt anyone. In fact, paying them attention and being involved will be that determining factor in how they view you when they are adults. Now all parents are not perfect, and I have even made some mistakes with Daisy and the twins during their childhood. But I am always very sweet to my children and I always give them lots of kisses and hugs. I don't want them to ever question my love or feel they were missing something. I always compliment them and I want them to be confident. I am trying my hardest to break generational curses and therefore I invest my all into my children. Don't let time fly by and you have kept yourself busy with everything else and have not given them the time they need.

For whatever reason rather it is your career, your friends, going out, the club, or even a smoking habit; don't let it consume your life away from your children. It is not worth it and you will be the very reason why your children will be raised with regrets. I don't ever want my children to say my mom didn't do this or didn't do that therefore, I invest a lot in my children. The worst thing a woman can do is put a man that is not her husband in front of her children. The reason I say this is because only when a man is your husband, should he go first. If you are guilty of this, change it now because if you break up with that man, and nothing is guaranteed, you lost out on quality time with your children that you cannot get back ever! So, love your children and do it more often. Children are indeed our future and it is important to be there for them no matter what. People say a million things about me, but they cannot say that I am not a damned good mother because I am the very best and my children can attest to this.

Women also should learn how to love their man properly. Men should learn to love their women right. Many women are mouthy, curse a lot, and very disrespectful to their men and wonder why they are not happy. There are certain things I don't do and I never have ever called any man I ever had out of their name. I am very respectful. If you get to that level just leave and do you and him a favor. It is not worth it if you lost respect and now you are being disrespectful.

Also, this advice is for the bitter baby moms out there and I am so sorry I must go in on you. If a man doesn't want to be with you, thank him. He would just cheat on you and make your life miserable. But, if he has moved on and now is a better man, it is perfectly fine. See, he might not be ready for what you were ready for at the time you were ready. Do not compare yourself to the new woman even if you think she is prettier or uglier than you. All that matters is that she is not for you, she is for him. So please don't keep the children away from him or use them as a pond because what you are now doing is making the children resent you and now you are creating painful memories for the children on how they were raised. We cannot break generational curses with bitter baby mothers out there. Allow them their parent time and move on. While he has the children, go find you a new man and better yet, take a vacation. You are officially on break! Enjoy it!

For the men, please don't start creating a new family and forget about your children. Always get them, take care of them, and include them in every way possible. If you take one family picture without them in it, you are hurting them. I dealt with this in my childhood and crazily it hurt me to see photos that I wasn't included in. So, please avoid this at all cost because if it is a daughter you are hurting you could be pushing her into the arms of a little non-deserving boy and that is always not good. So please love your children enough to pay close attention to what you are doing. When you leave their mother, you are leaving them regardless of how you feel. You can always tell them you love them and visit but life for your child is no longer the same. Life for them has changed forevermore and you leaving is now a part of their story and they will tell everyone that their father is not there. Don't be a statistic! Remember that absence does not make the heart grow fonder, it raises awareness of neglect.

Learning how to love your children and significant other is one thing, but also learning to love your family is a whole other topic. Many people mistreat their very own family because they feel as though that they will be there no matter what because of the bloodline. But do know how you treat people can change their lives forever. Growing up I experienced many things and most of the pain I had was from family. My very own brother has hurt me more than any man. I know many people would never publish anything relating to family pain in fear of the outcome but, as a culture, we got to stop the madness. This is my story to tell and if someone doesn't like what I put out, they should have thought about what they did to me and know that every person needs an outlet. Some people do nothing, some stay depressed, some even commit suicide, but my outlet is writing.

I hate that as a culture we cannot talk things out and work out our issues with each other. We need to change that and create outlets to enhance communication in our families. Every family has family secrets and I refuse to tell all of the secrets but I will discuss what happened to me. I decided to write this book for so many reasons, but also for self-help for many women or men who went through pain while being raised. Hopefully, someone who is going through something out there in the world can relate. Everyone always looks at me and thinks that I have a perfect life. Well, I am here to tell you I don't. I grew up poor, raised all by myself, for the most part, lost my virginity at

13, got pregnant at 15, delivered my first and only biological child at 16, my child's father cheated on me with a close friend, I been through a divorce, I got serious daddy issues, I adopted my brother's children which resulted in my brother and I not communicating properly or should I say at all for now 8 years, I had to start completely over and sold everything, and I lost almost all my friends along the way. But, for some reason, I am still smiling and pushing myself along the way.

There is nothing perfect about me, but I do have God and with him, I learned a lot about myself. I had an unfortunate beginning. I ended up with many scars along the way. I moved so much it changed me. I have been a huge disappointment to my family at one point. I have been through so much pain being foolish with my decision on men. I had to start completely over and go through a full storm alone. I dealt with the absence in men in my life. I adopted twins in which changed my life for the better but the story behind it caused division in my family and pain. I had to learn to love again and even what love means. I took my time healing which is the only way I am sane today, and I learned so many lessons along the way that I can now share with each of you.

The point of sharing is to let you know that it is okay not to be perfect. It is perfectly fine to have a past that is shattered and that has caused you so much grief. But what is important is that you learned from it and learned to move on. You have to learn to forgive yourself for the many bad decisions you made and be conscious of the decisions you will make. I was fortunate to turn out like how I did, even with all the challenges in my life. I think that even though it was extremely rough and I couldn't see any light at the end of the tunnel. I learned a lot about how I think and how I do things. I learned about what I need to do in the event I am ever faced with any future unexpected issues.

Growing up without a functional

family wasn't the ideal life for me or anyone. But, there are always lessons that coincide with pain. I might have been independently raised, but the good news is I earned something no one can ever take from me and that is my INDEPENDENCE. There is nothing like knowing that me, myself, and I can and will do all things with Christ who strengthens me. Now that I am in a new relationship, I am very careful and making better decisions. Do know that you haven't heard the last of me. I am always motivated to do more, and I hope that I inspired some folks to do more with their life and make some necessary changes. It is not hard you just have to find the strength and get to it. Whatever moves you to inspire change, will help you grow. Do not let your past define you, because you can grow. I know this because I had a rough start in my life but, I have always been Independently Moved! Stay tuned...

Meet the Author

D r. Erika Jones was born on the south side of Chicago. Throughout her childhood, she moved around a lot living in mostly the south suburbs. She became a mom at the early age of 16. Being a teen mom motivated her to push for success. She skipped a grade in high school going from a sophomore to a senior and went straight to college. She received her Bachelors of Art in 2007, her Master's in Public Administration in 2009, and her Ph.D. in Public Policy & Administration in 2018. She is raising 3 beautiful girls. She spends her spare time advocating for social justice, writing, and reading books. Her career of choice is Finance/ School Administration and has been for the last decade.

Keynote

A young, successful African American
woman who accomplished so much
in life early on in her career. But,
suffered severely in secrecy throughout
her childhood from always being
unaccompanied. Growing pains came
with a cost before it became rewarding.

Printed in the United States
By Bookmasters